SOUTHWEST SCROLL SAW PATTERNS

SOUTHWEST SCROLL SAW PATTERNS

Patrick Spielman & Dan Kihl

STERLING PUBLISHING CO., INC.
NEW YORK

Library of Congress Cataloging-in-Publication Data

Spielman, Patrick E.
   Southwest scroll saw patterns / by Patrick Spielman and
Dan Kihl.
        p.   cm.
   Includes index.
   ISBN 0-8069-0679-0
   1. Jig saws.   2. Woodwork—Patterns.   3. Woodwork—
Southwestern States—themes, motives.   I. Kihl, Dan.
II. Title.
TT186.S6747   1994
745.51—dc20
                                                              94–20413
                                                                 CIP

                    3   5   7   9   10   8   6   4   2

               Published by Sterling Publishing Company, Inc.
                 387 Park Avenue South, New York, N.Y. 10016
                    © 1994 by Patrick Spielman and Dan Kihl
                    Distributed in Canada by Sterling Publishing
               % Canadian Manda Group, One Atlantic Avenue, Suite 105
                         Toronto, Ontario, Canada M6K 3E7
                 Distributed in Great Britain and Europe by Cassell PLC
                 Villiers House, 41/47 Strand, London WC2N 5JE, England
                Distributed in Australia by Capricorn Link (Australia) Pty Ltd.
             P.O. Box 6651, Baulkham Hills, Business Centre, NSW 2153, Australia
                      Manufactured in the United States of America
                              All rights reserved

                      Sterling ISBN 0-8069-0679-0

Contents

Color section follows page 32.

Introduction

This book provides nearly 240 all-new scroll-saw patterns inspired by the great early cultures of the American Southwest. Each design has been developed and refined by scroll-sawing expert Dan Kihl, who actually earns his livelihood cutting out and selling these well-tested designs.

Almost every design has historical significance. Many images depict actual Native American ways of life and ceremonial traditions that are several thousand years old. A number of patterns are copies of petroglyphs (carvings on rocks), sand paintings, drawings made on pottery, and other archaeological findings from various early Native American nations of the Southwest.

The interest in, and demand for, woodworking projects and cutouts incorporating designs of the Southwest is rapidly growing. The Southwestern style has become popular not only across the United States but throughout the world. It is definitely the "in" motif of today's interior decorators.

In this book, you will find a variety of new, quick, and easy patterns to use for various projects for homes decorated in the Southwestern style. You will find patterns that can be incorporated into functional projects as well as patterns that are intended purely for decoration.

Engage your imagination to incorporate these designs into such functional woodworking projects as letter/napkin holders, pegboards, clocks, welcome or name signs, jewelry boxes, shelves, tie and key racks, wastebaskets, lampshades, magazine holders, pedestals, tissue dispensers, kitchen furnishings, and other household accessories.

We encourage you to maximize the use of these patterns. Consider choosing different materials and enlarging or reducing the sizes to satisfy individual needs and desires. Because photocopiers are now so accessible to almost everyone, we've included some tips on how to use them quickly and efficiently to size a pattern to any dimension. With the photocopying technique, you'll be able to easily custom-size a pattern to fit your own needs.

In addition to using natural or painted solid woods and plywoods of various species and thicknesses, you can make these cutouts from soft metals, plastic, and leather to match your own decor and color scheme. Designs can be pierced or sawn through to provide a silhouetted opening, or they can be cut out, painted, finished, and then glued onto a backing as an overlay.

You will find many of the patterns printed in our new two-tone shading. The darker areas indicate optional overlays or areas that can be inlaid, wood-burn-shaded, painted, or given other special treatment to add more variety and visual interest to your workpieces. Dan Kihl makes extensive use of two different techniques for finishing copper, explained in the following section.

Thin sheet brass and even the aluminum from recycled beverage cans make excellent overlay and inlay material, or you can simply use metallic paints.

If scroll sawing is new for you, we recommend *Scroll Saw Basics* (see page 157); this book covers essential instructions for scroll sawyers and how to use scroll saws to make basic cuts. We have included some general scroll-sawing tips in *Southwest Scroll Saw Patterns* along with some techniques for inlaying contrasting materials. Refer to *Scroll Saw Handbook* for more extensive information about making inlays and cutting non-wood materials.

—Patrick Spielman

Metric Conversion

Inches to Millimetres and Centimetres						
MM—millimetres				*CM—centimetres*		
Inches	**MM**	**CM**	**Inches**	**CM**	**Inches**	**CM**
⅛	3	0.3	9	22.9	30	76.2
¼	6	0.6	10	25.4	31	78.7
⅜	10	1.0	11	27.9	32	81.3
½	13	1.3	12	30.5	33	83.8
⅝	16	1.6	13	33.0	34	86.4
¾	19	1.9	14	35.6	35	88.9
⅞	22	2.2	15	38.1	36	91.4
1	25	2.5	16	40.6	37	94.0
1¼	32	3.2	17	43.2	38	96.5
1½	38	3.8	18	45.7	39	99.1
1¾	44	4.4	19	48.3	40	101.6
2	51	5.1	20	50.8	41	104.1
2½	64	6.4	21	53.3	42	106.7
3	76	7.6	22	55.9	43	109.2
3½	89	8.9	23	58.4	44	111.8
4	102	10.2	24	61.0	45	114.3
4½	114	11.4	25	63.5	46	116.8
5	127	12.7	26	66.0	47	119.4
6	152	15.2	27	68.6	48	121.9
7	178	17.8	28	71.1	49	124.5
8	203	20.3	29	73.7	50	127.0

Basic Tips

The Southwestern projects presented in this book are by and large fun, fast, and easy to make. Making these cutouts requires no great artistic talent nor any special equipment (other than a scroll saw and a drill to make holes for sawing inside openings). No special sawing or advanced woodworking skills are required. In fact, any boy or girl beyond the age of eight or nine can easily learn the basics of scroll sawing and will soon be able to make an array of projects to keep or to give as gifts. Many of the patterns can also be cut with a band saw, but youngsters and beginning woodworkers shouldn't use this machine without complete instructions and constant supervision. The scroll saw is much safer than the band saw, and it's easier for everyone to learn to use.

A number of the patterns are designed for simple cutouts. Some of these very same patterns have areas indicating where optional advanced inlay work can be performed. Wood burning, painting, or simply applying thin overlays to these areas are other options.

Sizing Patterns with a Photocopier

Most communities have copy shops, but photocopiers with enlarging capabilities can also be found in public libraries and schools. Check the Yellow Pages of your telephone directory under the heading of "Photocopying" or "Copying" for the shop nearest you. New photocopiers are capable of enlarging any original pattern from this book to any size up to 200 percent, in one-percent increments. And you can get even greater enlargements by simply enlarging an already enlarged photocopy. The cost of making a photocopy of a pattern from this book is minimal (usually just a few cents). Having a photocopy made is quick, convenient, and far more expedient and accurate than the other old-fashioned ways of copying or enlarging patterns that use the squared-grid system or pantograph tracings.

Enlarging with a Proportional Scale

A proportional scale (see Illus. 1) is an inexpensive device that can help you determine exactly what percentage of enlargement or reduction you will need to set the photo-

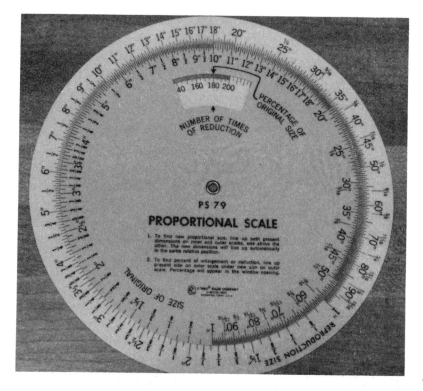

Illus. 1. An inexpensive proportional scale, such as the one shown here, makes enlarging or reducing patterns to a specific size with a photocopy machine quick and precise. It actually tells you what percentage to set the photocopy machine at to get a pattern of a predetermined size.

copier at to produce a pattern of a specific size. The scale is very easy to use; all the little numbers and divisions make it look much more complicated than it really is. This device is simply made up of two rotating discs, with numbers around their perimeters, joined by a common pivot. Align the dimension you have on one disc with the dimension you want on the other. The exact percentage at which you will need to set the copy machine will appear in the opening. This process eliminates guesswork and trial-and-error methods from the sizing process. It also saves you money spent on wasted photocopies. Proportional scales are found in art-, graphics-, and printing-supply stores. Check the Yellow Pages to locate a shop that sells these helpful devices.

Wood—Material and Thickness

A number of the patterns in this book will result in very fragile cutouts if sawn from solid wood. Notice the example of the Kokopelli key-rack project (Illus. 2). In such cases, a good grade of plywood, such as Baltic birch or other hardwood plywood, is recommended rather than solid wood, because of its inherent-strength advantage. Many of the fretted silhouette patterns are also best sawn from thin plywoods, unless they are to be used as overlays and glued to solid backers. The best material and thickness are a matter of choice, availability, and functional need for the intended end use. Generally, thin plywood, 1/4" or less, is satisfactory for some of the hanging projects with ornate fret-type cutouts. Solid wood usually has better visual appeal and generally is the best choice, providing it will be strong enough for the use at hand.

Transferring Patterns to the Wood

Transferring patterns to material for sawing can certainly be done in traditional ways, such as tracing with carbon or graphite papers. However, the new technique just involves the following steps: 1. copying the pattern directly from the book on an office-quality copy machine, at which time it can be enlarged or reduced as desired; 2. cutting out the pattern with a scissors to a rough size; 3. coating the back of the pattern with a very light mist of temporary-bonding spray adhesive (Illus. 3); and 4. hand-pressing the pattern copy directly onto the workpiece.

Temporary-bonding spray adhesives are available at crafts shops and from mail-order sources. One kind we use is 3-M's Scotch Brand Spray Mount Adhesive, but other brands work equally well. Some craftspeople prefer using a brush-on application of rubber cement for securing patterns to the workpiece. This is an effective technique only when working with small paper patterns.

Before using, test the adhesive on scrap first. To use the spray adhesive, simply spray a *very* light mist onto the back of the pattern copy—do not spray it on the wood.

Illus. 2. This key rack made from the Kokopelli flute-player design incorporates an inlay. The project is cut from ⅜" plywood with a decorative inlay of solid wood.

11

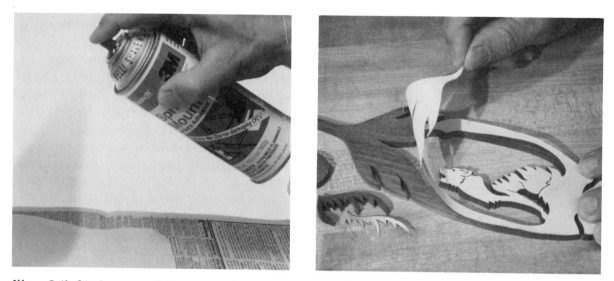

Illus. 3 (left). An aerosol temporary-bonding adhesive is used to coat the back of the pattern. Note that the pattern is cut to a rough size and newspaper catches the overspray. Illus. 4 (right). After you've finished sawing, remove the pattern. The paper should peel off easily without sticking or leaving any residue on the wood surface.

Wait 10 to 30 seconds, and then press the pattern onto the workpiece. It should maintain contact during sawing. After all the cutting is completed, the paper pattern should peel very easily and cleanly from the workpiece (see Illus. 4). Should the pattern be difficult to remove because too much adhesive was used, simply wipe the top of the pattern with a rag slightly dampened in solvent.

Definition Cuts

This is a sawing technique specified on many patterns to make the completed project appear more realistic and detailed. The process involves making a single kerf, or interior saw cut, through the work to represent a certain feature or effect. (See Illus. 5 and 6.) Only pinless-type saw blades can effectively be used for making interior, single-line definition cuts. This age-old fretwork technique of making single-line cuts was widely used by scroll sawyers more than a hundred years ago. Definition-cut lines can originate entirely within the design itself or be cut by sawing inward from the outside edge.

Generally, this work is done with fine, thin blades, but the actual size used de-

Illus. 5. Here is an example of the effective results that can be achieved with definition cuts.

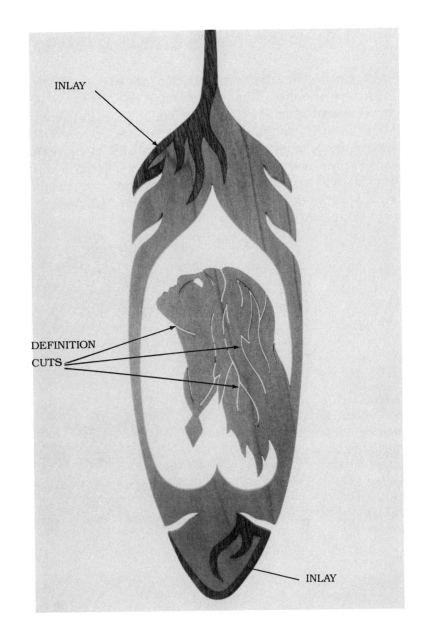

INLAY

DEFINITION
CUTS

INLAY

Illus. 6. Indications for definition cuts and inlays of solid wood are shown here. Definition cuts are single-width saw kerfs that originate within the design itself or are cut by sawing inward from the outside edge.

pends on the thickness of the material and the character of the line being cut. Interior definition cuts are most effective when the entry hole for the blade is barely large enough to permit the blade to be threaded through the workpiece. A 3⁄64"-diameter hole will allow the use of a No. 4 scroll-saw/fretsaw blade. A 1⁄32"-diameter hole allows a No. 2 blade. If the material is very thin, try using a sharp knife to make a very narrow, undetectable slit for blade entry.

Here's a scroll-sawing tip: Sharpen the end of the blade to a point so that it can be forced into a hole that is smaller than the usual size. This will make the blade-threading area almost totally undetectable.

Surface-detailing lines can also be applied with a wood-burning tool. Painted or sealed wood can be lined with ink, or soft-tipped felt markers can be used. These methods are especially advantageous when using scroll saws that carry pin-type blades.

13

Stack Sawing

Stack sawing is a basic production technique that should not be overlooked whenever a quantity of the same cutout is required. Stack, or plural, cutting involves sawing two or more layers of materials at the same time. Very thin plywood can be stacked to as many as 17 or more layers and cut all at once. Sometimes scroll sawyers will use an inexpensive, low-grade material as a bottom layer to prevent saw-blade tearout, or feathering, from occurring on the bottom or exit side of the project itself. (See Illus. 7.) Layers can be held together in various ways while they are sawn, including nailing (Illus. 8) or tacking, spot gluing in the waste areas, and using double-faced tape.

Illus. 7. This photo shows stack sawing six layers of 1/16" plywood to be used as overlays. Note the use of the inexpensive 1/4" plywood backer under the stack to prevent tear-out, or feathering, along the exit side of the cut of the bottom layer.

Illus. 8. Stack sawing is an effective production technique by which a number of identical pieces are all cut at the same time.

Using Metals, Plastics, and Leather

As mentioned earlier, a variety of different materials can be used for the patterns in this book. Soft steel up to about ⅛" thick can now be cut fairly easily with modern constant-tension scroll saws equipped with metal-cutting blades (see Illus. 9). Thin

Illus. 9. Here is a Kokopelli figure sawn from soft steel and spray-finished. The copper-colored spray finish with glitter makes this an eye-catching piece. The same effect can be achieved using painted plywood.

metals—such as brass, copper, and aluminum—available at crafts shops can also be used (see Illus. 10). Material of this type can be utilized in two different ways. It can be sawn out and used as a separate overlay bonded directly onto the surface of a cutout profile, such as shown on the lizard in Illus. 11. Or, thin metals can be bonded to inlay stock (preferably to a plywood material) with contact cement or a permanent-bond spray adhesive. This material is stack- or bevel-sawn and then inserted (inlaid) into an opening cut through the design profile.

Almost any pattern can be cut from wood with thin metallic overlays or plastics. Several projects incorporate mirrored plastic as either backers or bases. Using mirrored plastic as backers against scenic silhouette designs creates a very stunning effect. Check your Yellow Pages under "Plastics" for local sources. Colored tagboard or fabrics of contrasting colors are good substitute backer materials that will enhance silhou-

Illus. 10. Thin, soft metals—such as brass, aluminum, and copper—make interesting overlays. Use contact cement or a spray adhesive for bonding.

ettes if mirrored acrylic plastic is not readily available.

Thin metals, thin plastics, and leather are best used bonded to plywood before cutting. All can be bonded with a contact cement or spray adhesive. Illus. 12 shows a pair of coyotes cut from leather bonded to plywood. In this project, the rough surface was placed outward. Also, note that two different kinds and colors of leather were incorporated into the design by employing basic inlaying techniques.

Illus. 11 (left). This metal-laminated plywood lizard cutout features a metallic decorative accent. In this case, it is a cutout metal overlay bonded to the surface. Illus. 12 (right). These are cutouts with contrasting-color inlays of leather bonded to plywood. The rough sides were placed outward for texture and visual interest.

Accents of Natural Materials

Stones, twigs, branches, hollow sections of logs, feathers, driftwood, and weathered boards are some of the natural materials that can be used to support or frame a cutout, making it a one-of-a-kind work of art. (See Illus. 13 and 14.) Usually the cutout needs to be nailed, stapled, or glued to keep it in position. Use an epoxy or a hot-melt glue when gluing wood to non-wood surfaces.

Segmentation

This is a fairly simple sawing process that can often be employed to add interest to a cutout. Essentially, all you do is cut the object into various parts, or component pieces. Then stain or paint the pieces differently and glue them back together in their original position to make the whole. (See Illus. 15.) Segmentation is a good alternative technique to inlaying or overlaying.

16

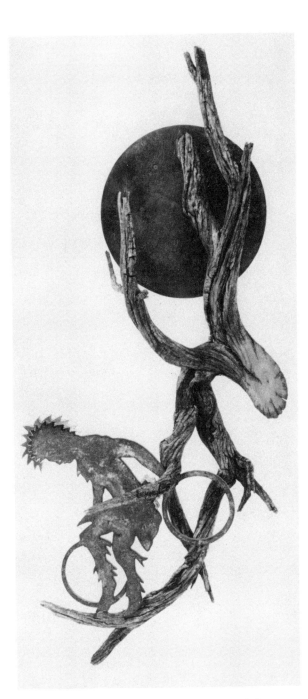

Illus. 14. The end-of-the-trail design is incorporated into a section of a hollowed log.

Illus. 13. This hoop dancer, cut from ⅛" plywood, has a metallic-headdress inlay and is mounted to a weathered branch from a dead tree. A brightly finished, orange copper disc glued to the wood branch simulates the sun.

Illus. 15. This project was originally cut from one piece of wood. Dark stain was applied to segmented horns and feather parts before gluing them back—a process that creates visual interest.

17

Inlaying

Inlaying is any process employed to decorate or adorn another surface by the insertion of another material. In scroll sawing, this is usually a contrasting material in color or type. Inlaying scroll-sawn projects can be done in two different ways.

The first and the easiest is the stack-cutting, or pad-cutting, method. This simply involves stacking two or more pieces of unlike material, color, or species together and then cutting various pieces, or components, apart from the whole at the same time. Then you interchange the pieces as you glue them to complete the whole again. (See Illus. 16 and 17.) The keys to this technique are to use as fine a blade as you can and to be sure that your saw table is adjusted perfectly square to the blade.

One problem associated with the stack, or pad, method of inlaying is that, upon close examination, the saw kerf may be visible in certain areas (see Illus. 18). This problem can be alleviated by using a bevel sawing–inlaying technique, but it also has its disadvantages.

Bevel sawing–inlay work is a more advanced technique and one that generally wastes more material. Its objective is essentially to fit the mating pieces together so

Illus. 17. This shows one of the two resulting projects from the stack sawing in Illus. 16. This one shows poplar with the darker mahogany inlays. Not pictured is a mahogany project with poplar inlays.

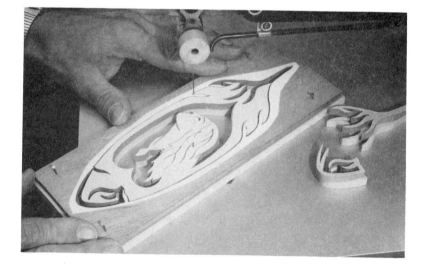

Illus 16. Here, ¼"-thick mahogany and poplar are being stack-sawn. Use a fine blade (No. 2 or finer), and be sure that the table is perfectly square to the blade. Notice, at the right, that the inlay pieces to be interchanged are already cut free.

18

tightly that no space at all is evident from the saw-kerf glue line. This can be accomplished by tilting the table slightly, somewhere between one and 10°. The exact amount of table tilt depends upon the cutting width of the saw blade (kerf size) and the thickness of the stock to be cut. The amount of bevel is most easily determined by trial and error. To give you an idea of how the bevel sawing–inlay technique can be applied to the patterns in this book, we have illustrated the major steps of a typical example. See Illus. 19–22 and the completed project in Illus. 2. Refer to the *Scroll Saw Handbook* for more information about making solid-wood inlays and other inlay, relief, or sculpturing techniques that can be employed with the scroll saw and many of the patterns in this book.

Illus. 18. Some visibility of a glue-filled saw kerf may be evident in some areas, as shown here, when employing the stack-sawn, or pad-sawn, method of inlaying.

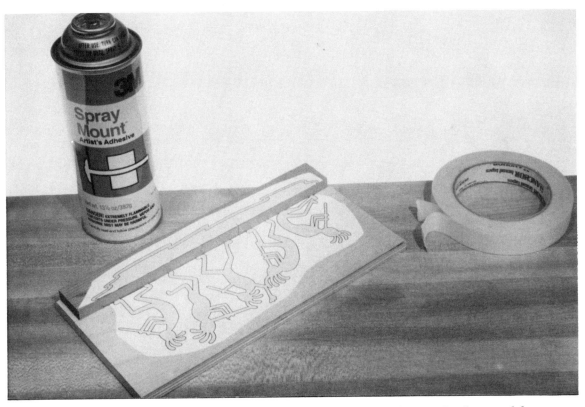

Illus. 19. Step 1. This step involves preparing the inlay and workpiece background for simultaneous bevel sawing. Here, ⅜" redwood is positioned on top of ⅜" Baltic birch plywood and secured with small pieces of double-faced tape. Note that the pattern copies are applied to both pieces with temporary-bonding spray adhesive.

19

Illus. 20. Step 2. With the saw tilted approximately 3½° to the right, saw around the inlay, feeding the work into the blade in a clockwise direction.

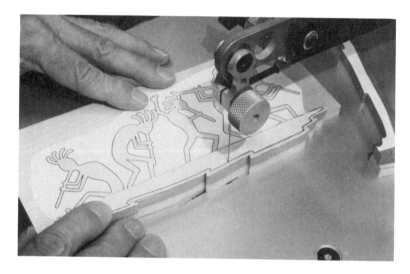

Illus. 21. Step 3. Continue sawing all around the inlay, feeding the material into the blade in a clockwise direction.

Basic Finishing Tips

Baltic birch, some other hardwood plywoods, and solid softwoods often do not stain well. Usually the problem is that some areas take the stain and other areas do not, so that you end up with an uneven, blotchy look. The key is to make an adequate test on a sizable piece of scrap before staining. Fretted hardwoods and some hardwood plywoods are best just dipped and then wiped dry; this is followed by blowing away excess finish from definition cuts and tight corners with compressed air. Usually we prefer not to stain and, in some cases, to just leave Baltic birch and some other woods unfinished.

We like penetrating oils, such as Danish oil, for woods that look best with a natural finish. As a rule, we avoid varnish and other glossy surface finishes.

Obviously, the choice and method of finishing are your decisions. Spray finishes often work great for scroll and fret cutouts. Baltic birch painted black can take on the look of metal, and metallic finishes can be

Illus. 22. Step. 4. Glue the inlay in place. and sand the surfaces flush after the glue sets.

used as well. You can also add glitter (refer back to Illus. 9) or, for a softer look, apply flock to surfaces.

A number of projects in this book show materials overlaid and inlaid in copper finished in two different ways. (See Illus. 23 and the photos in the color section.) Usually the entire project, including the inlay, is made of very thin, bright copper laminated to ⅛ or ¼″ Baltic birch. After all the sawing is completed, the inlay is lacquered before it is glued in place to maintain the bright, new copper look. The surrounding area or body is soaked in an acetic-acid bath to oxidize the surface and change the shiny copper to an aged look called patina or ver-

digris. This is a beautiful bluish-green deposit that can be formed not only on copper but on brass and bronze surfaces as well. The combination of the bright copper with the aged-looking bluish green is very striking visually, and this is certainly a new technique not yet common among scroll sawyers. Try this technique if you want to visually set your work apart from other scroll work.

You can also buy a "patina green finish." This is a chemical solution formulated especially for this effect. But we encourage you to experiment with your own oxidized finishes.

Illus. 23. The coyote is all cut from copper laminated to ⅛″ Baltic birch plywood. The shiny inlay areas (which appear dark in this black-and-white photo) are clear-lacquer finished. The body is soaked in an acetic-acid bath, which turns the copper a beautiful bluish green, creating a stunning contrast to the shiny copper-colored areas. (See the photo in the color section.)

Patterns

Bases for Sawn Figures

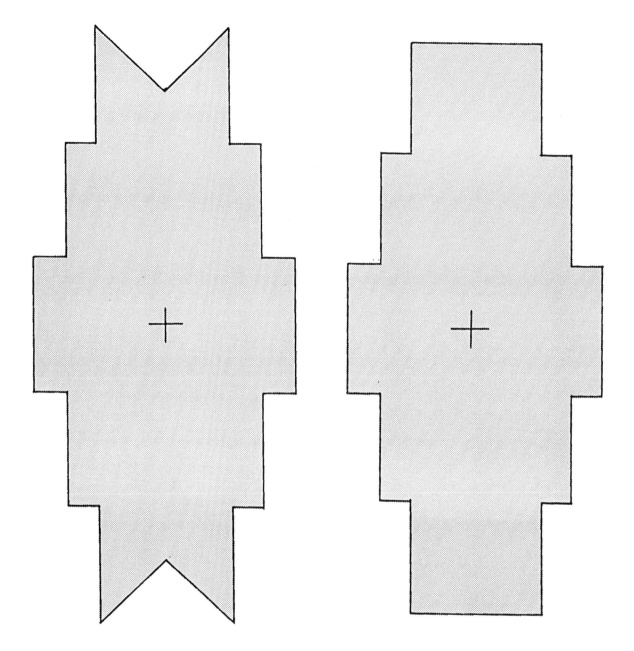

Bases in Southwestern designs for standing figures. Enlarge or reduce as appropriate.

24

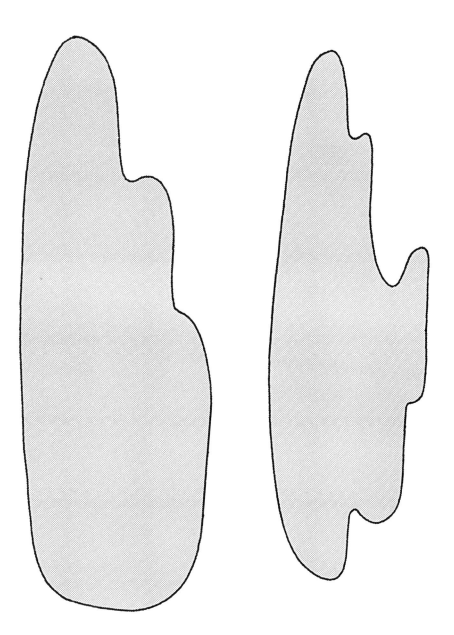

Free-form bases.

Kokopelli Designs

The legendary Kokopelli flute-player design dates back to around A.D. 200. It is a very well known figure in the Southwest and one of the most popular and significant of all Native American figures. Many early Native American tribes used this figure in pottery designs, petroglyphs, and pictographs. Many artists today feature or incorporate it in a variety of media and artistic expressions. This one was sawn from soft steel and spray-finished with a metallic-copper base coat and a copper-glitter top coat.

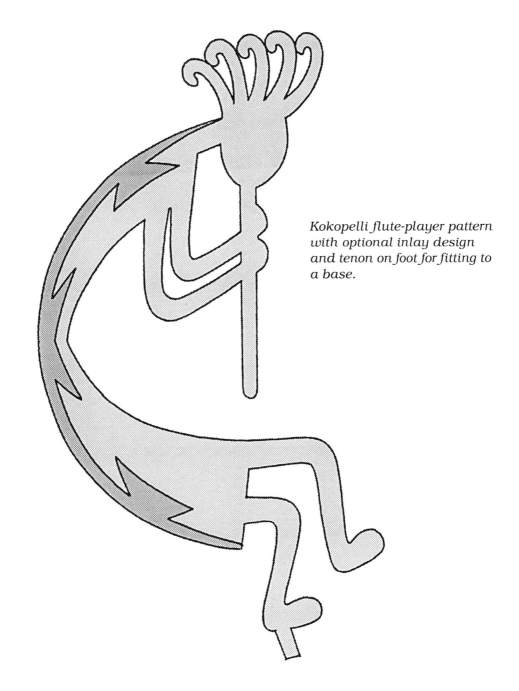

Kokopelli flute-player pattern with optional inlay design and tenon on foot for fitting to a base.

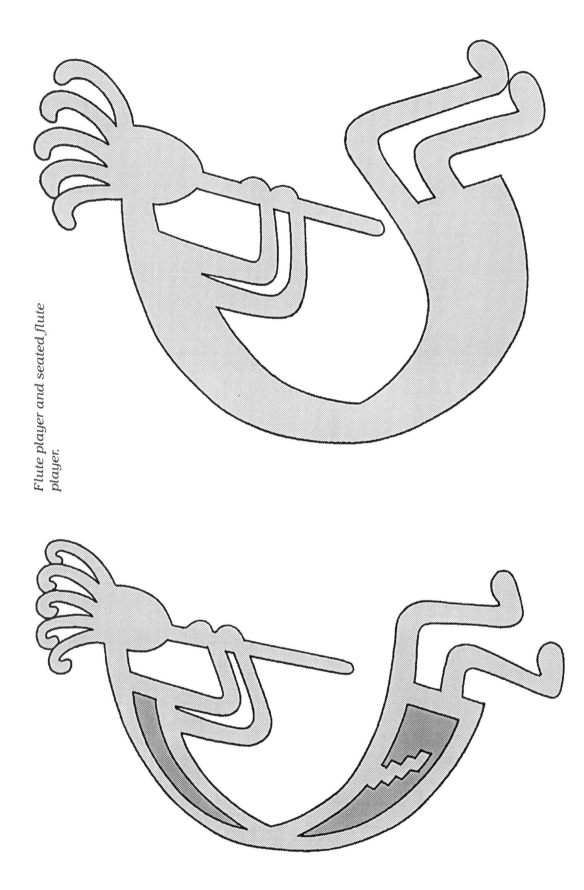

Flute player and seated flute player.

Five flute players.

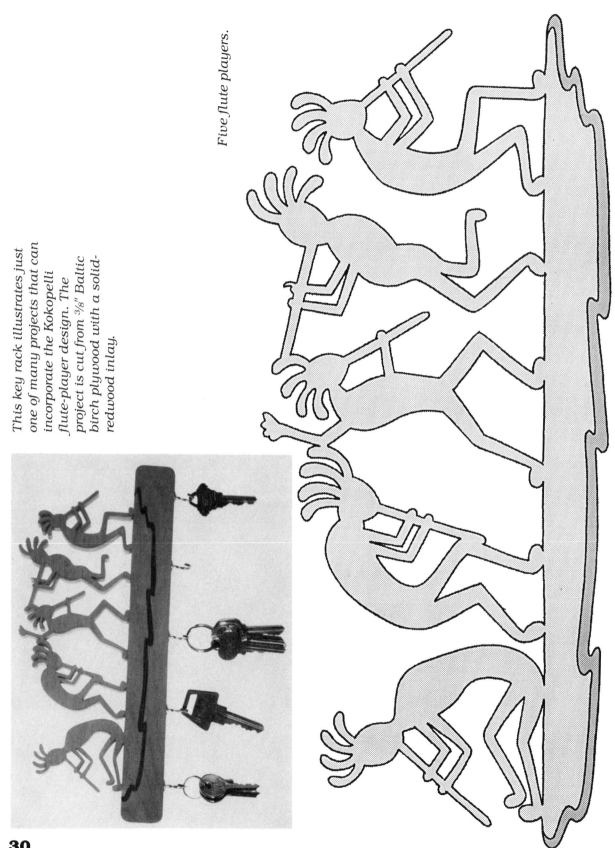

This key rack illustrates just one of many projects that can incorporate the Kokopelli flute-player design. The project is cut from ³/₈" Baltic birch plywood with a solid-redwood inlay.

Five flute players.

Miscellaneous Small Figures and Symbols

Mini-cutouts of ⅛" plywood
glued to round, mirrored,
acrylic plastic bases.

Mini-clock fit-ups 1⁷/₁₆" in
diameter fit into 1³/₈" holes
bored in solid blocks with ¹/₃₂"
plywood overlays.

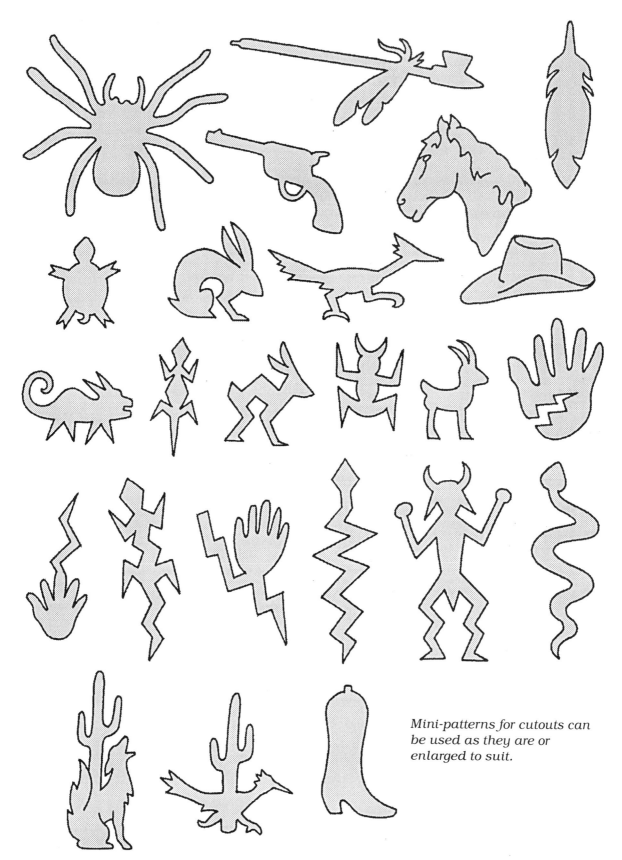

Mini-patterns for cutouts can
be used as they are or
enlarged to suit.

A pair of coyotes sawn and inlaid from leather glued to thin plywood (page 53).

Coyote of copper with acid-bath treatment and bright inlays (page 43).

End-of-the-trail design from thin copper laminated to ⅛-inch plywood is framed by natural log section (page 77).

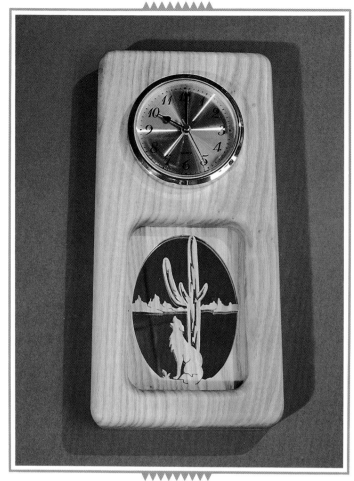

Ash wall clock (page 113). An acrylic mirror backs a silhouette scene sawn from ⅛-inch solid wood.

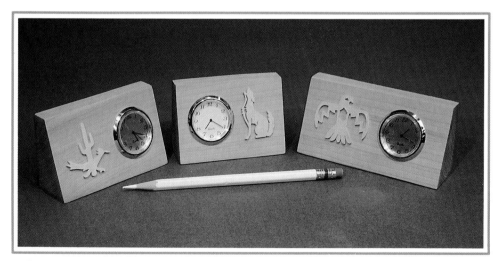

Mini quartz clock inserts fitted into hardwood blocks decorated with overlays sawn from ¹⁄₁₆-inch plywood (pages 31 and 87).

Kokopelli on a base finished with a copper-paint base coat with copper-copper glitter top coat (page 26).

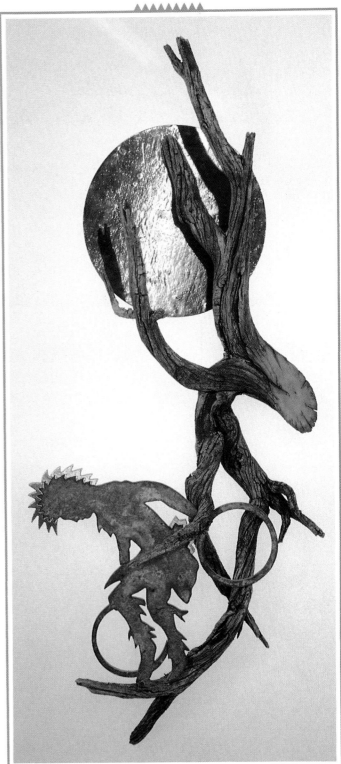

Hoop dancer and sun sawn of copper and mounted to weathered wood (page 65).

C

Silhouettes sawn from unfinished Baltic birch plywood (page 120).

Mimbre lizard design cut from ¹⁄₁₆-inch plywood stained and used as the overlay (page 148).

D

Buffalo of copper with acid-bath finish and bright inlays (page 68).

Kokopellis cut from copper (page 29).

Hummingbird on branch of acid-treated copper (page 106).

Segmented buffalo head with feathers sawn from one piece of ⁵⁄₈-inch solid oak (page 70). Horns and feather parts were stained dark before gluing in place.

Some cutouts of unfinished plywood (page 31).

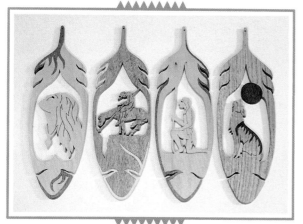

Feathers of ¼-inch hardwood with contrasting inlays created by the stack- or pad-sawing technique (pages 127–130).

F

Some mini cutouts of wood glued to bases of mirrored acrylic (page 31).

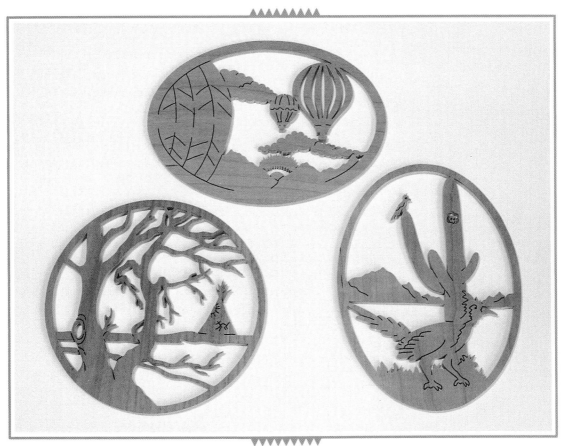

Scenic silhouettes cut from ¼-inch hardwood plywood (pages 110, 115, and 118).

Flocked-plywood pot design with copper overlaid to wood and then overlaid to the project (page 140).

Kokopelli key rack design cut from ³⁄₈-inch Baltic birch plywood with a solid redwood inlay (page 30).

Copper lizard (page 133). The body is finished with an acid-bath treatment and inlay is lacquered to maintain its brightness.

Thunderbird, owl, coyote, and sunset.

33

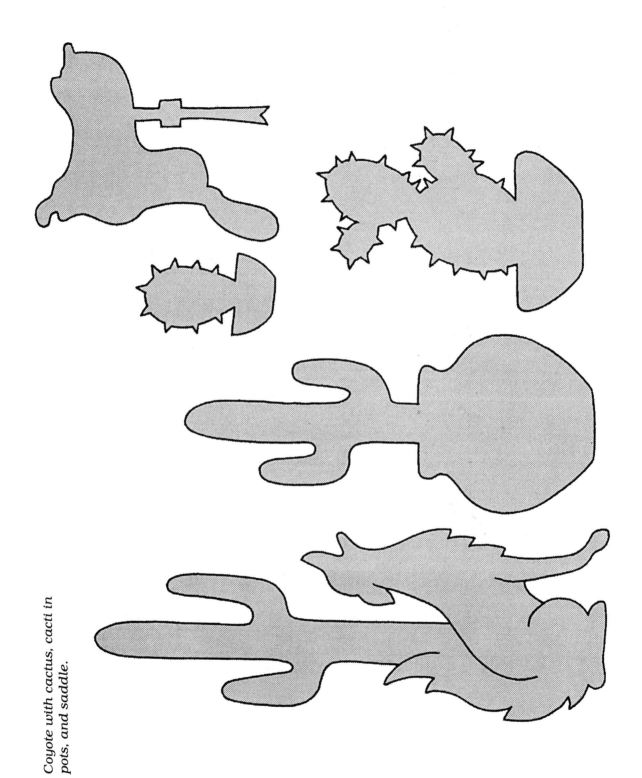

Coyote with cactus, cacti in pots, and saddle.

Horned toad, armadillo,
snake, buffalo skull with
feathers, and roadrunner
with its dinner.

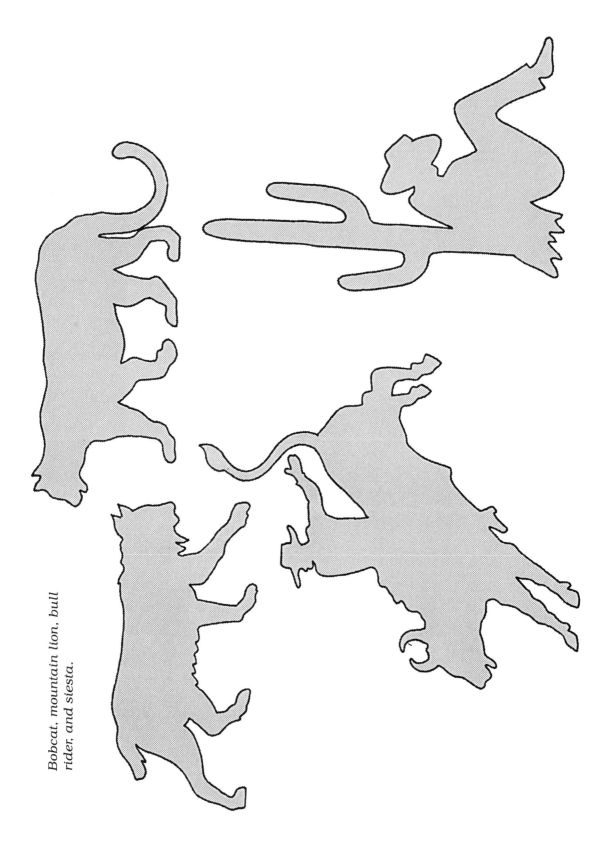

Bobcat, mountain lion, bull rider, and siesta.

Donkey, feather, eagle, two quail, and another eagle.

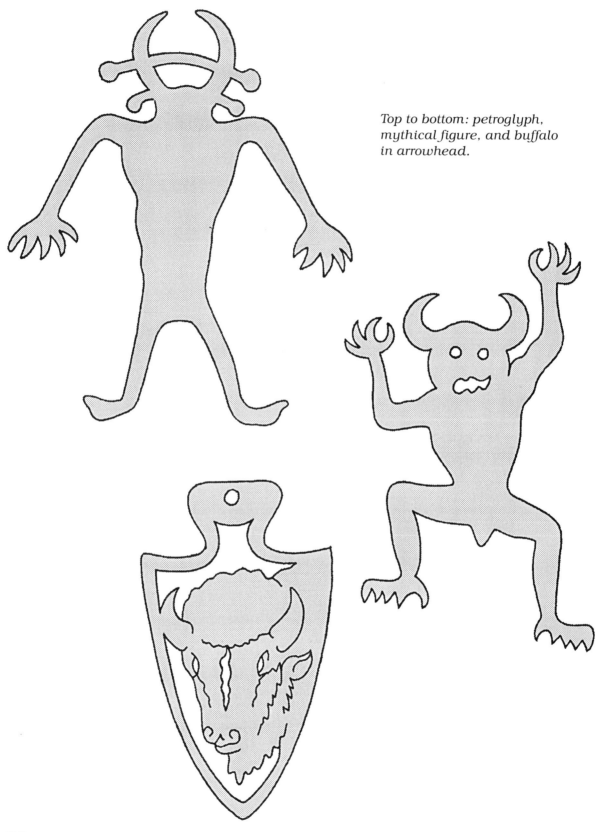

Top to bottom: petroglyph, mythical figure, and buffalo in arrowhead.

Kokopelli flute player, chili pepper, arrow through arrowhead, and coyotes.

39

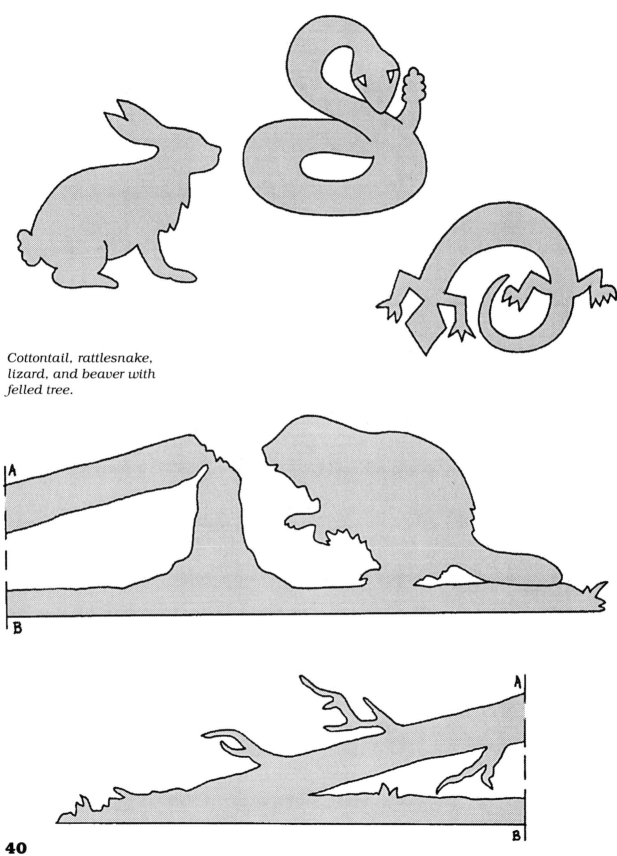

Cottontail, rattlesnake, lizard, and beaver with felled tree.

A

B

A

B

40

Bucking bronco and eagle.

Native American ceremony and lizard.

Coyotes

Coyote made of copper-laminated plywood, featuring acid-finished body with lacquer-finished inlays.

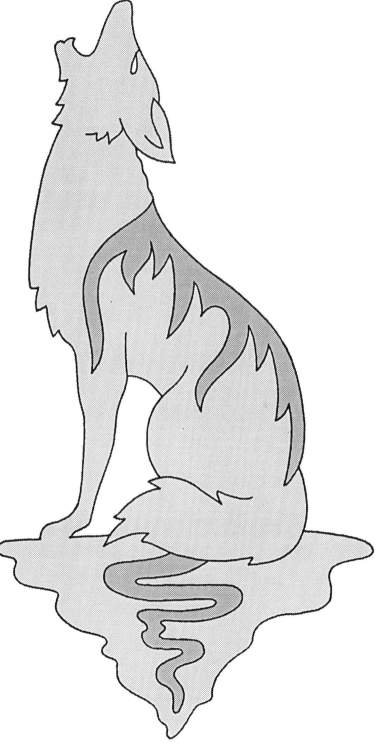

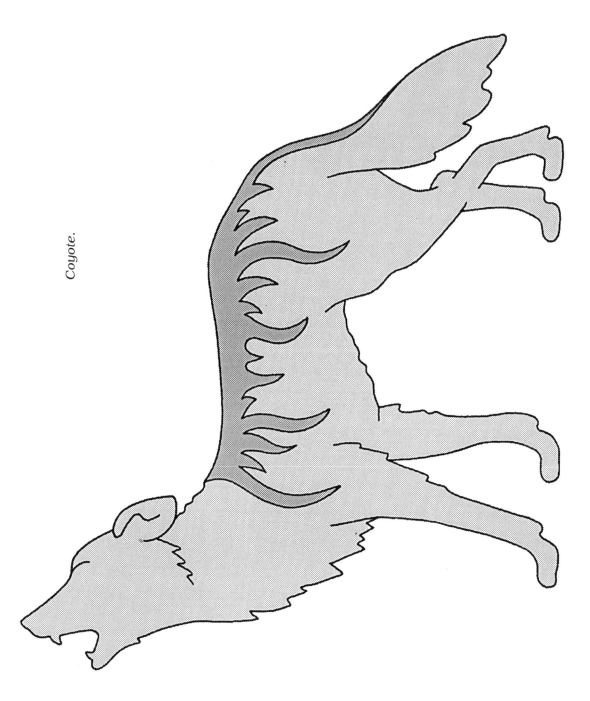

Coyote.

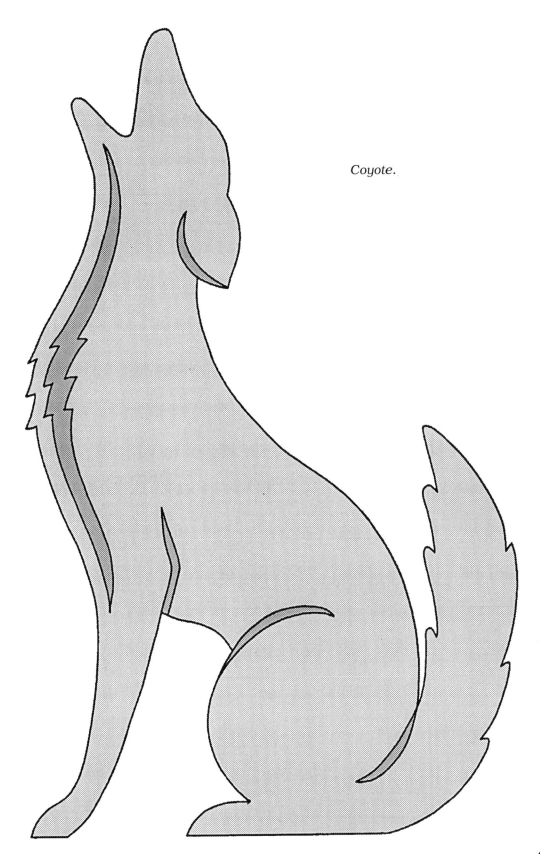

Coyote.

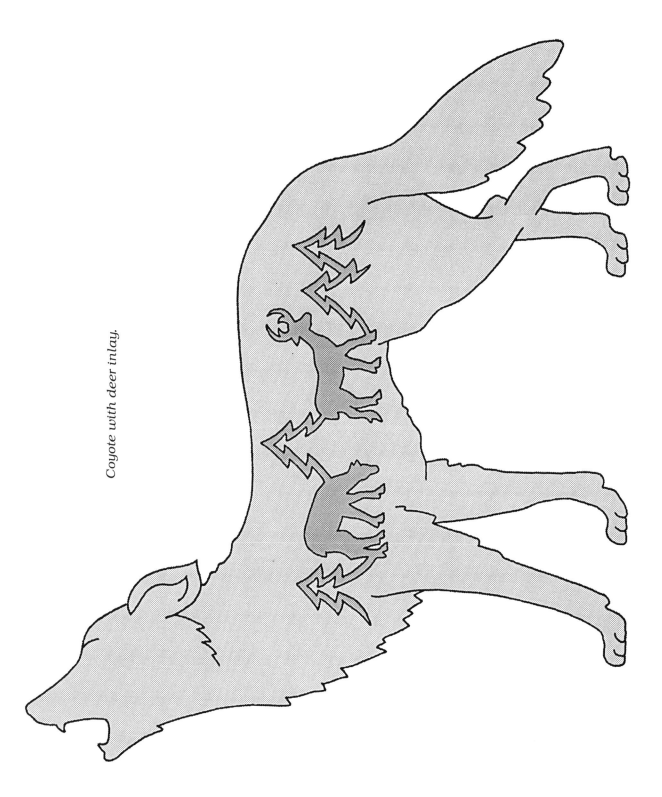

Coyote with deer inlay.

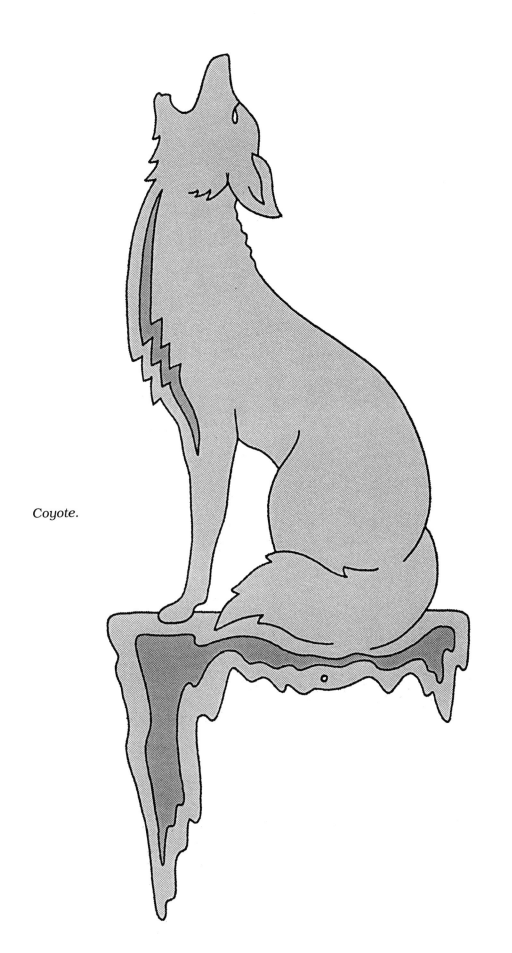

Coyote.

47

Coyote with cactus and moon.

48

Coyote in the moon.

A

B

Coyote with moon.

50

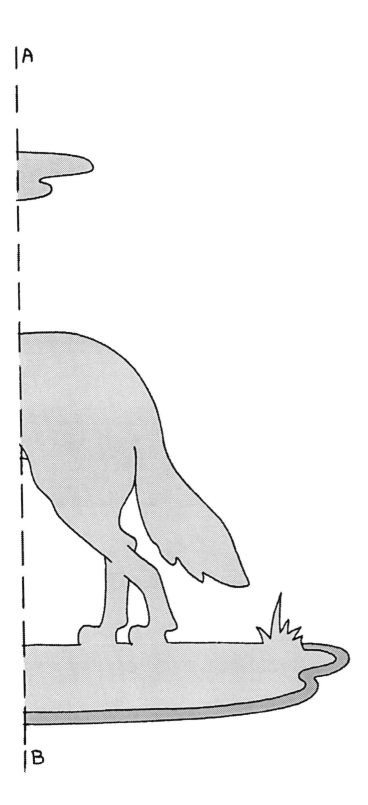

A

B

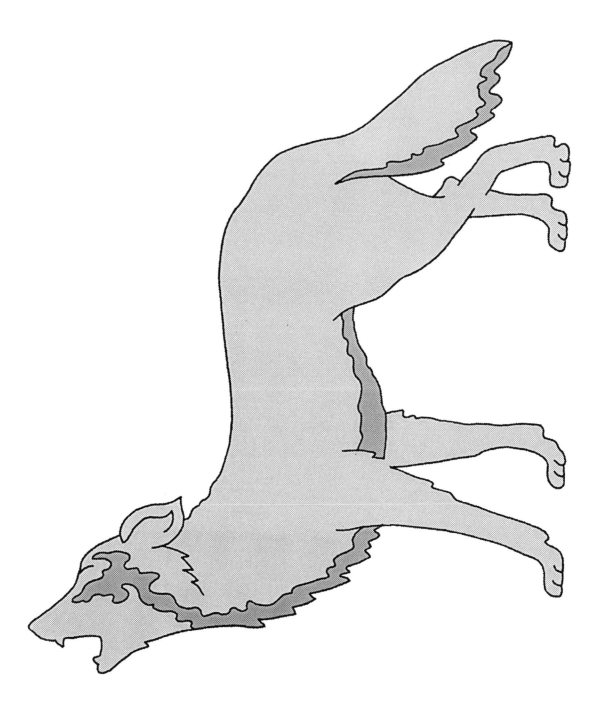

Coyote.

Coyote.

Coyote scene.

Native Americans

Native American scout.

Native American with pipe.

Native American woman and adobe.

Native American woman with feather in hair.

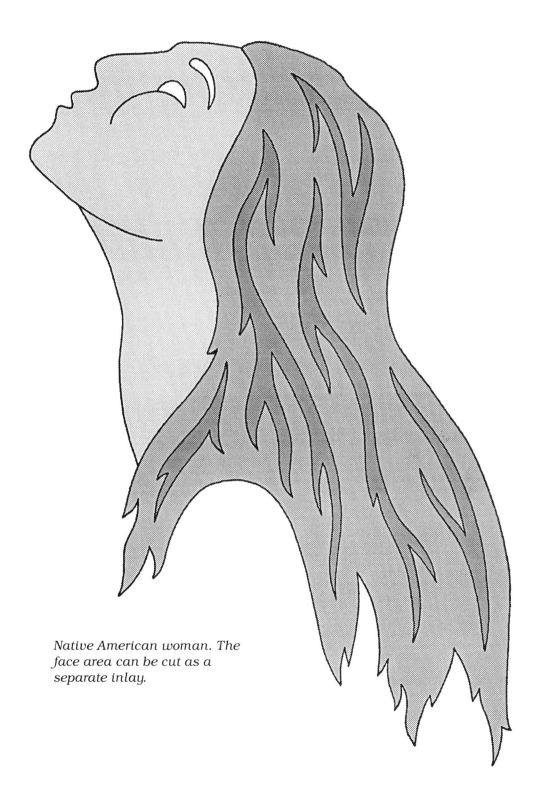

Native American woman. The face area can be cut as a separate inlay.

59

*Native American woman
painting pottery.*

60

Sun with face, tepee, and
camp scene.

Sun and eagle dancer.

*Native American with eagle
and buffalo head.*

Hoop dancer on weathered wood glued to copper sun.

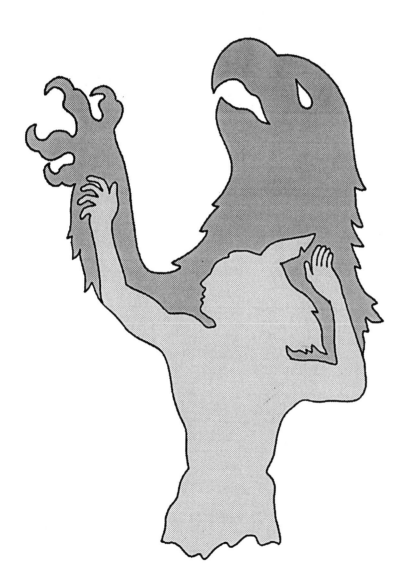

Native American and eagle.

Hoop dancer.

A

B

A

B

Buffalo, Elk, and Horses

Buffalo and donkey.

Native American watching buffalo.

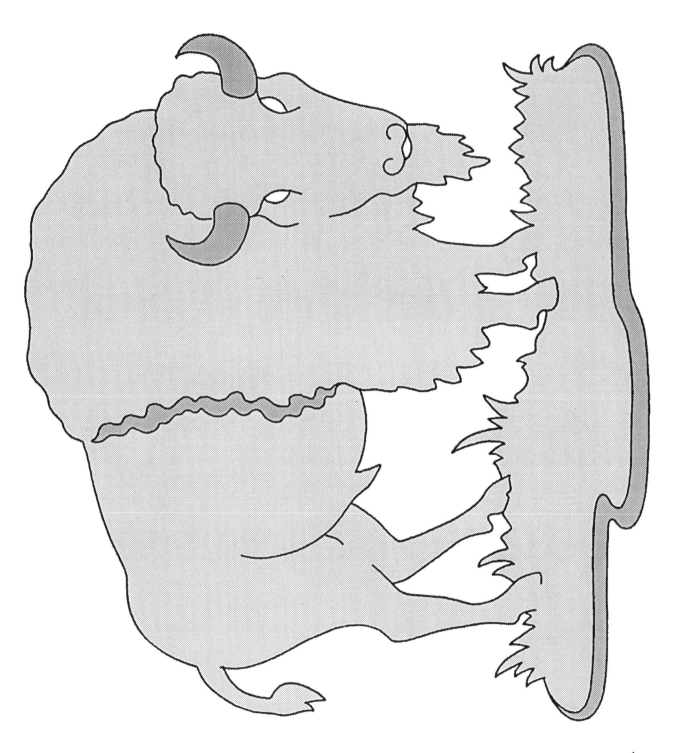

Buffalo.

Buffalo with buffalo skull.

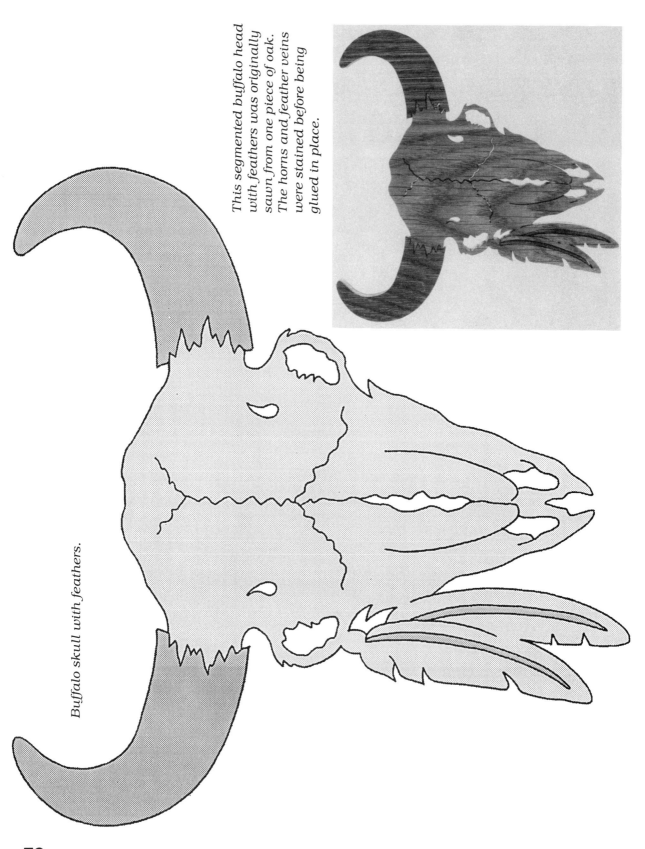

This segmented buffalo head with feathers was originally sawn from one piece of oak. The horns and feather veins were stained before being glued in place.

Buffalo skull with feathers.

70

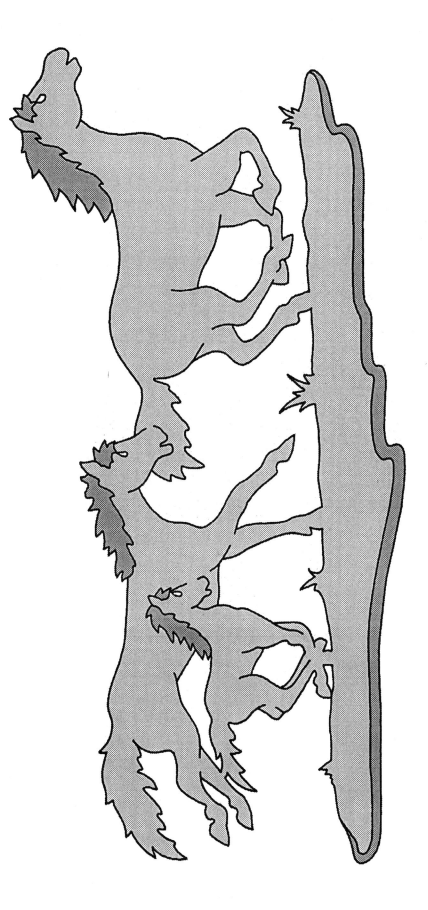

Horses running.

A

B

Buffalo hunt.

A

B

73

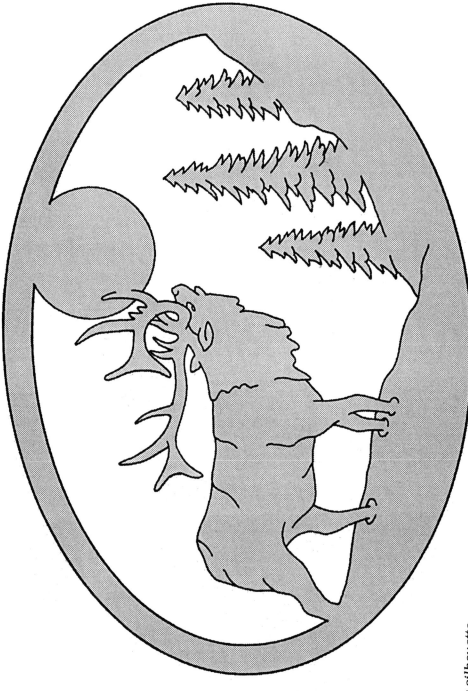

Elk silhouette.

Horse.

Elk and horse.

End-of-the-Trail Scenes

This project features the end-of-the-trail design. The horse has an inlay, and the sun is cut of copper laminated to ⅛" plywood and stapled to the back surface of the hollowed-log section.

End-of-the-trail design with inlay.

End-of-the-trail silhouette.

End-of-the-trail design with
several inlays.

79

*End-of-the-trail silhouette
with partial border and sun
inlays.*

80

Cowboys

Boot with spurs and rope frame.

*Cowboy with lasso, and
cactus with bird perched on
cow skull.*

82

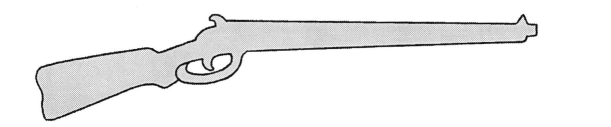

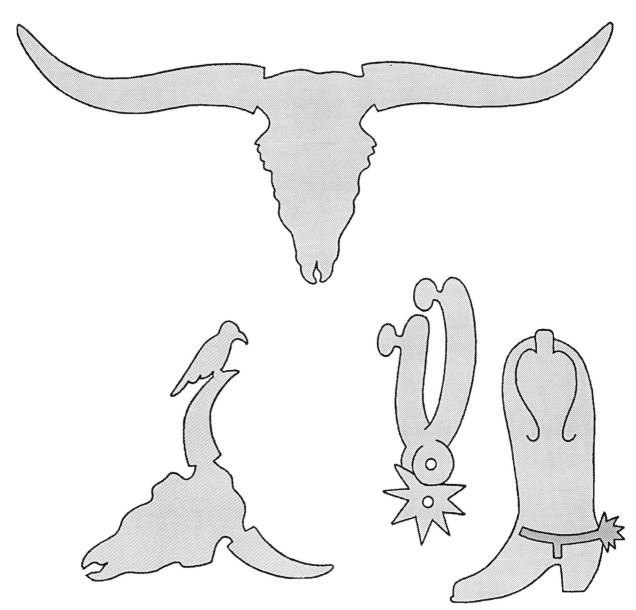

Rifle, long-horned steer, bird perched on cow skull, and spur with boot.

High-noon gunfight.

84

Cacti

Fetish bear, saguaro with bird, and saguaro with prickly pear.

Saguaro cactus and sun.

Cactus with quarter moon, prickly pear, cactus with full moon, roadrunner with cactus, and prickly pear.

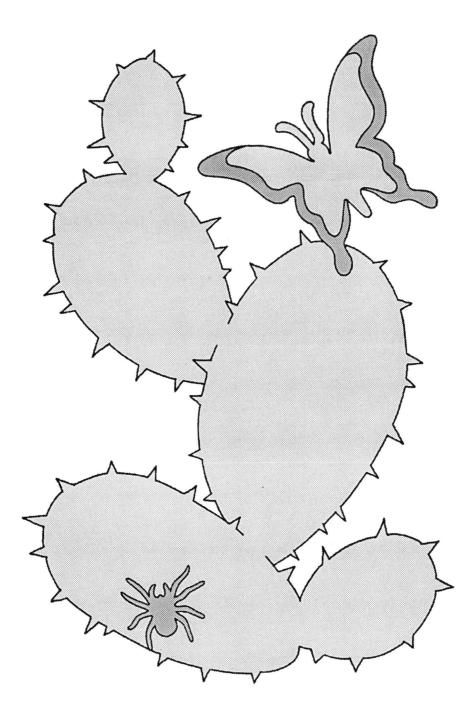

Prickly pear with tarantula and butterfly.

88

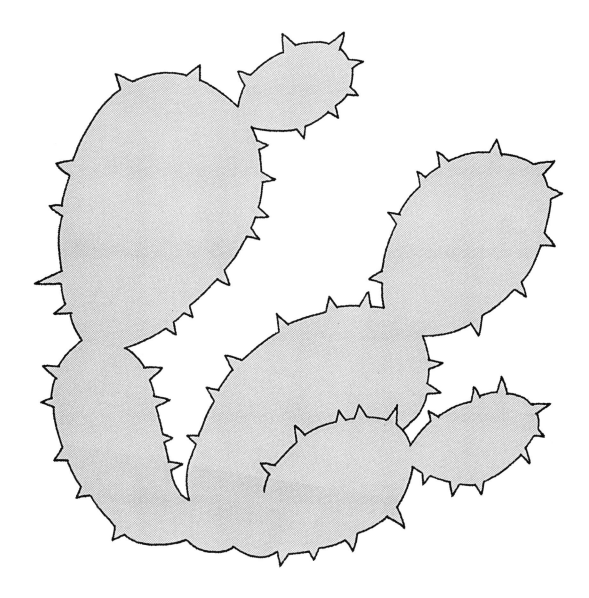

Prickly pear.

Coyote with cactus and bird.

90

*Grass (top), yucca (left), and
prickly pear (right).*

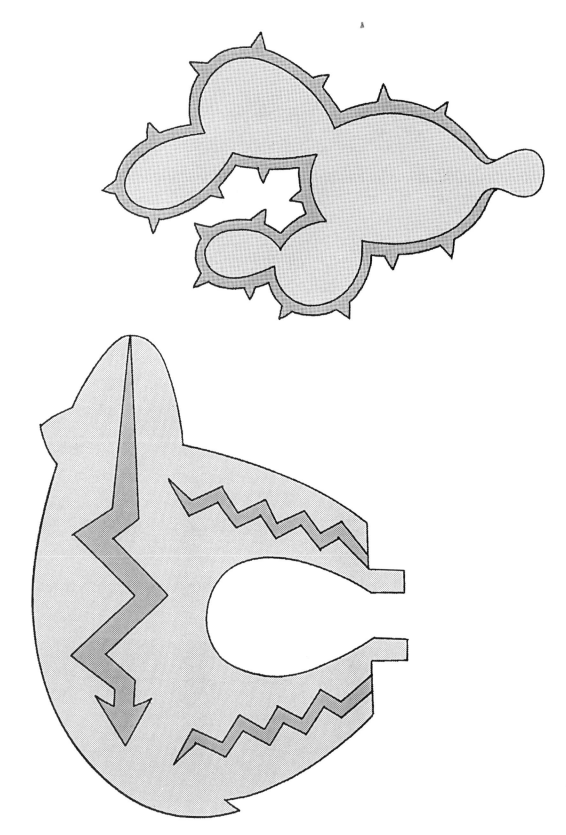

Bear and prickly pear.

Birds and Flowers

Cardinals.

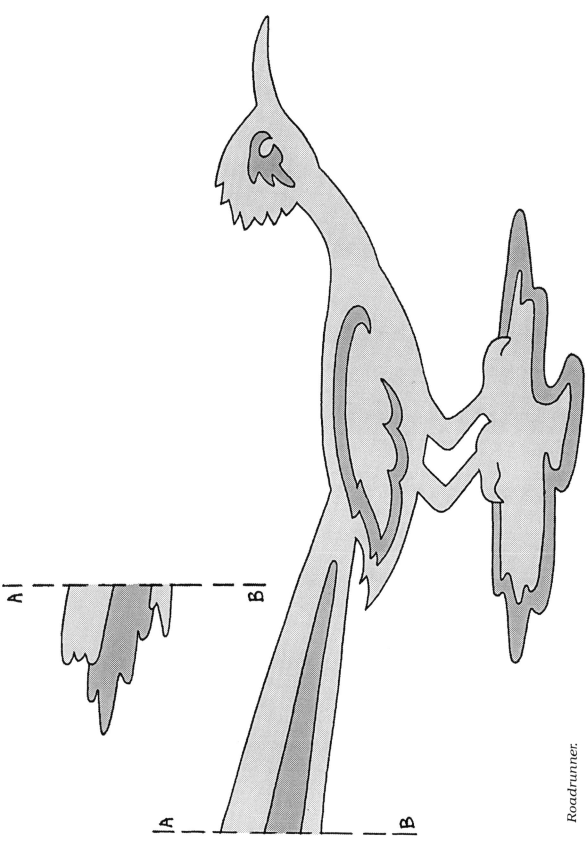

A   B

A   B

Roadrunner.

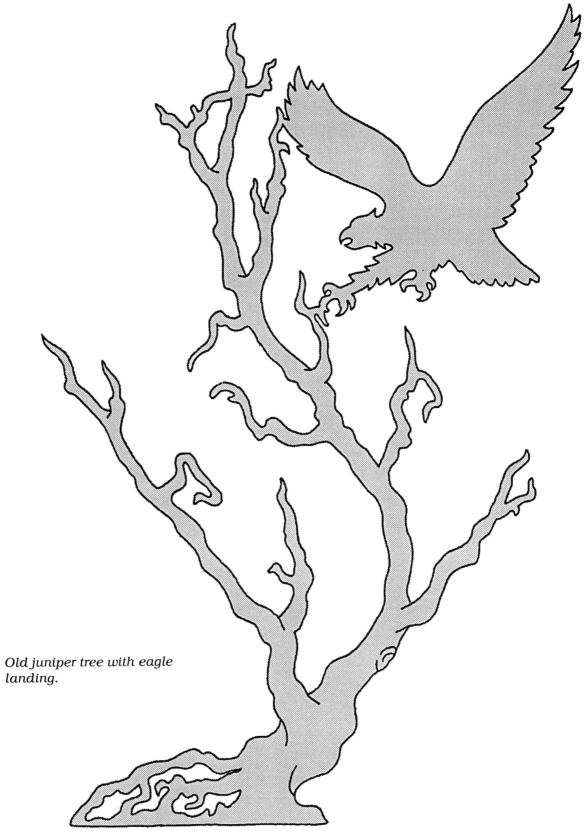

Old juniper tree with eagle landing.

95

Owls.

Owl-scene silhouette.

Eagle silhouette.

98

Eagle.

Quail with prickly pear.

Quail.

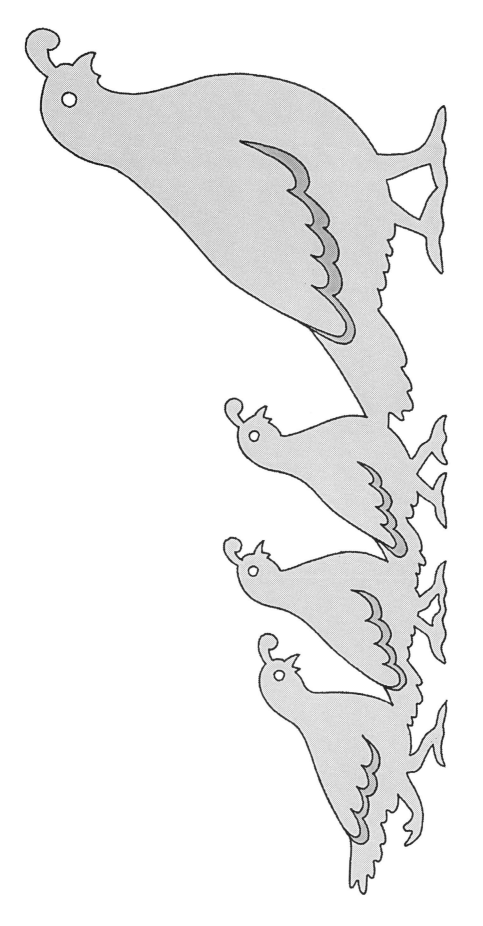

Quail family.

Quail, hummingbird, and owl.

103

Ducks in flight.

104

*Sitting hummingbird, and
hummingbird with morning
glories.*

105

Hummingbird on branch.

106

Hummingbird encircled.

Fancy hummingbird.

108

Eagle and rose.

Silhouette Scenes

Tree with tepee.

110

Sun with face.

Coyote-in-desert scene.

112

Here is one way to incorporate a silhouette scene or other design into a hanging wall clock. The ash body of this clock is machined from ¾ to 1"-thick stock. The scene is sawn from ⅛"-thick matching wood backed with ⅛"-thick acrylic plastic mirror stock. This project can be sized to suit, enlarging or reducing pattern(s) as desired, to be in proportion with the clock selected. (See the back view on the next page.)

113

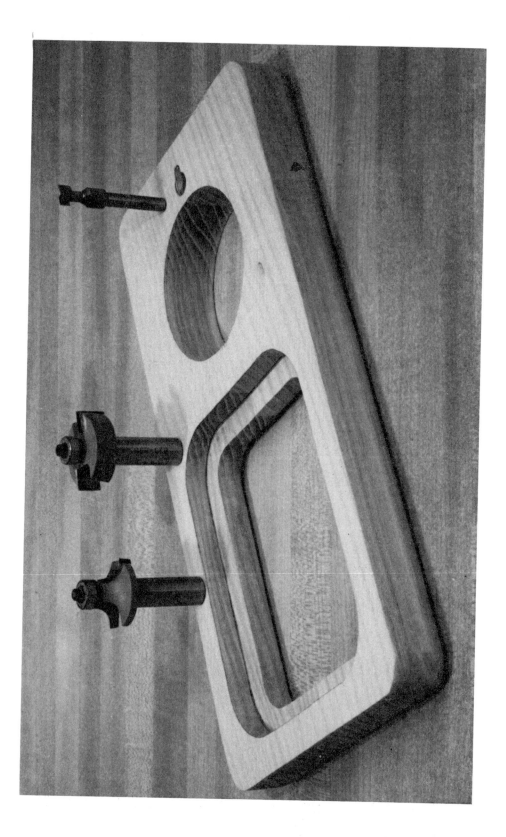

Back view of the wall-clock project and the router bits used.

Roadrunner scene.

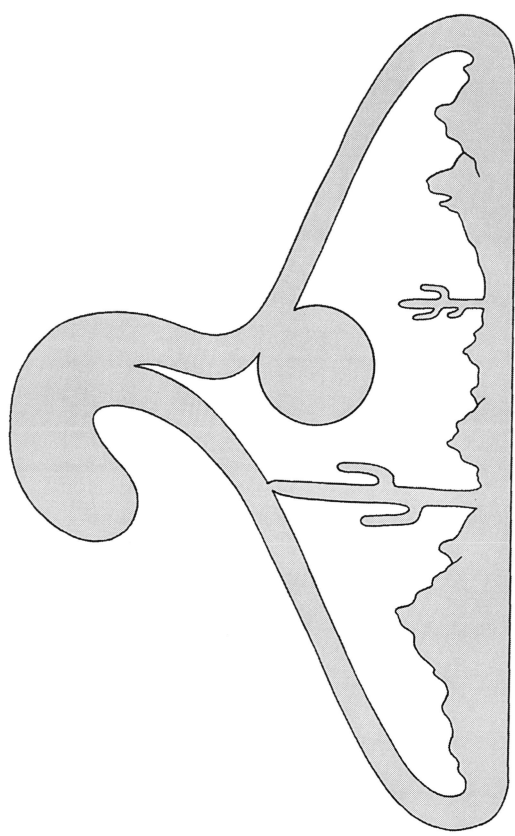

Southwestern-scene hanger.

Buffalo skull and hummingbird.

117

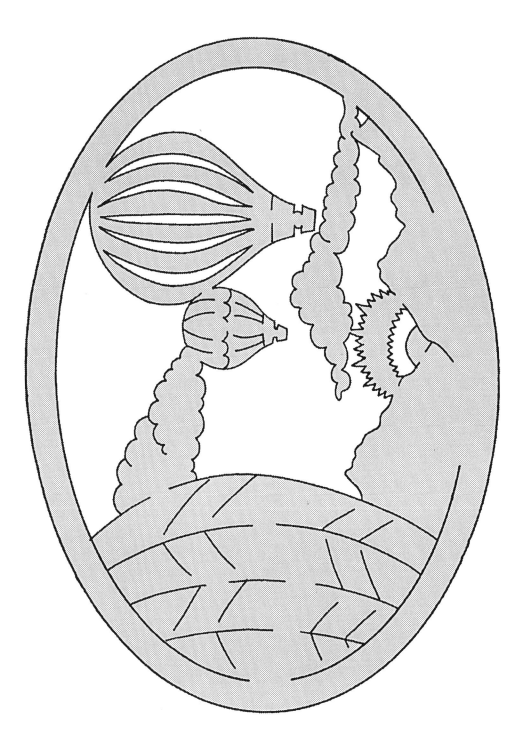

Scene of hot-air balloons.

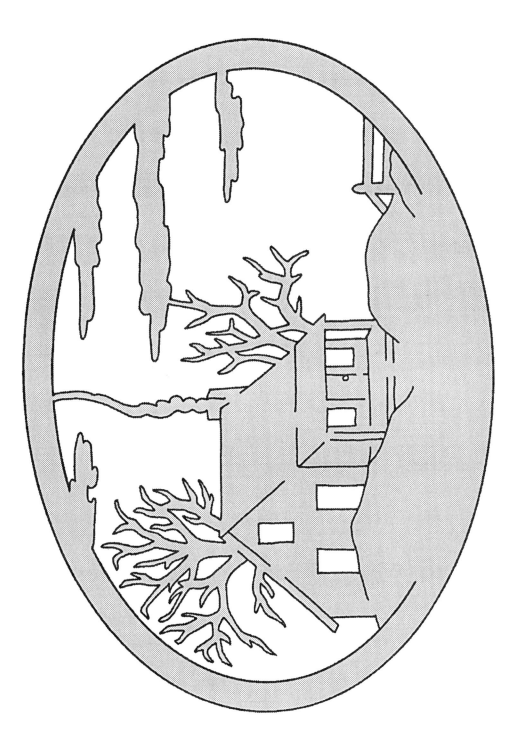

House.

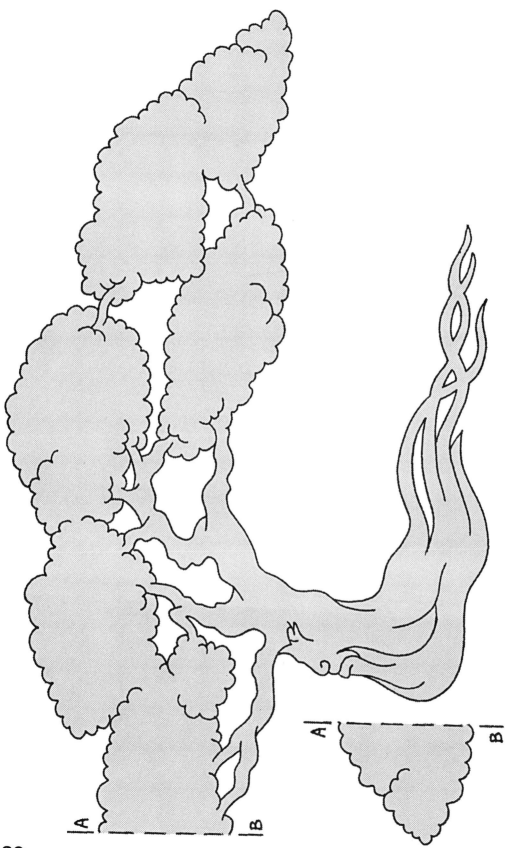

Old-man juniper (see page 122 for the finished project).

Owl flying off into the sunset (see the next page for the finished project).

Old-man juniper sawn from
¼"-thick Baltic birch
plywood.

Scene of owl flying into the
sunset, sawn from ⅜" Baltic
birch plywood.

122

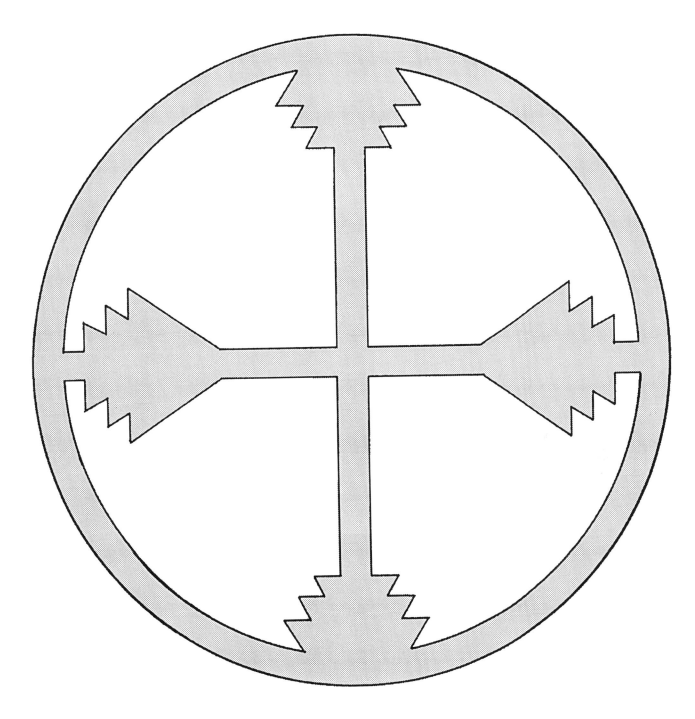

Southwestern-frame design.

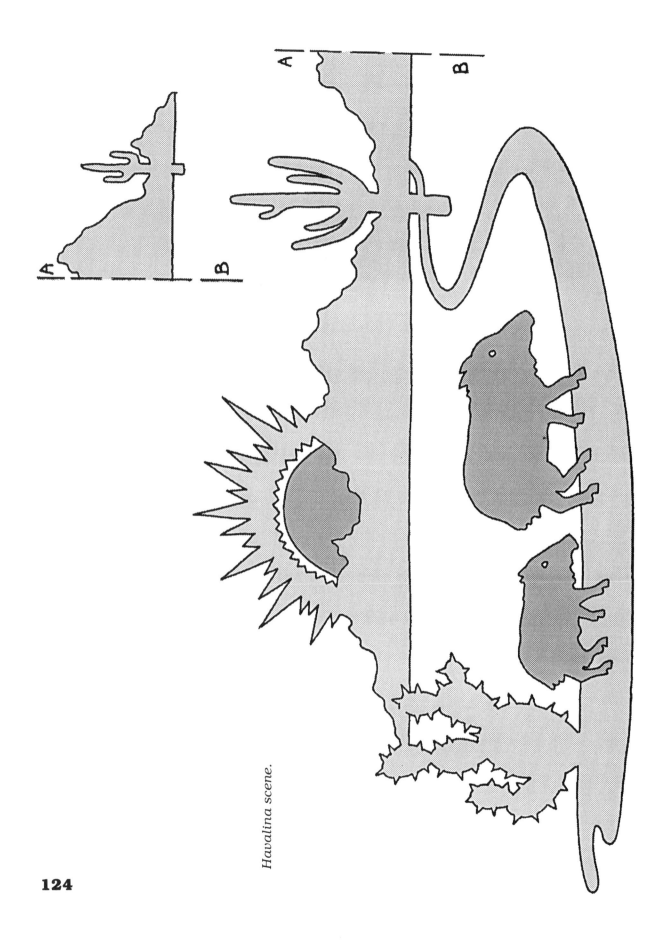

Havalina scene.

124

Antelope.

Feathers

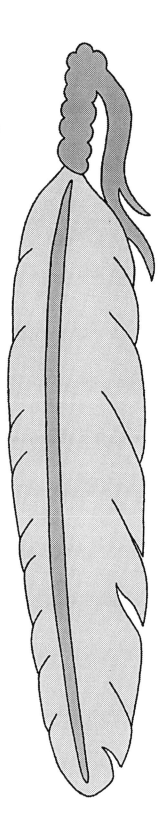

Feather.

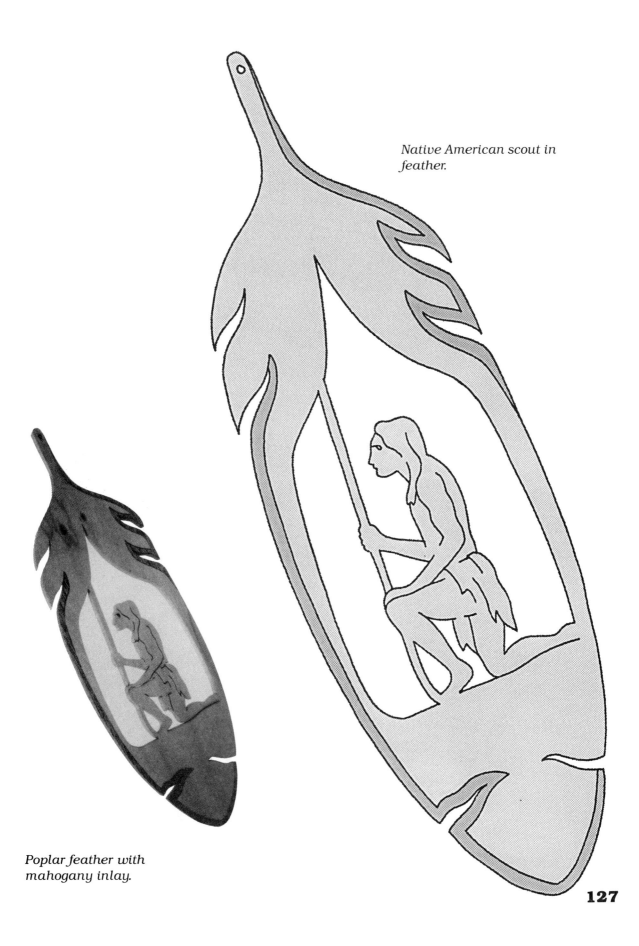

Native American scout in feather.

Poplar feather with mahogany inlay.

127

End-of-the-trail scene in feather.

Mahogany feather with poplar inlay.

128

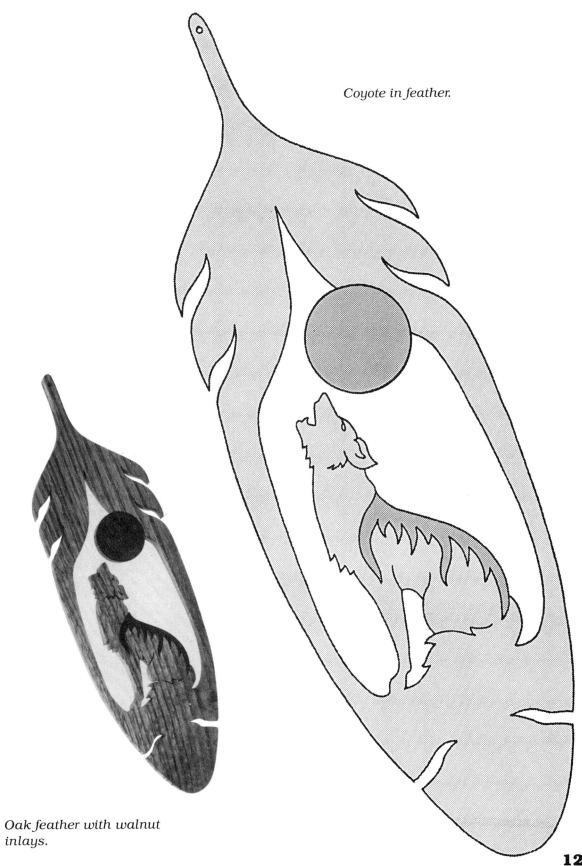

Coyote in feather.

Oak feather with walnut inlays.

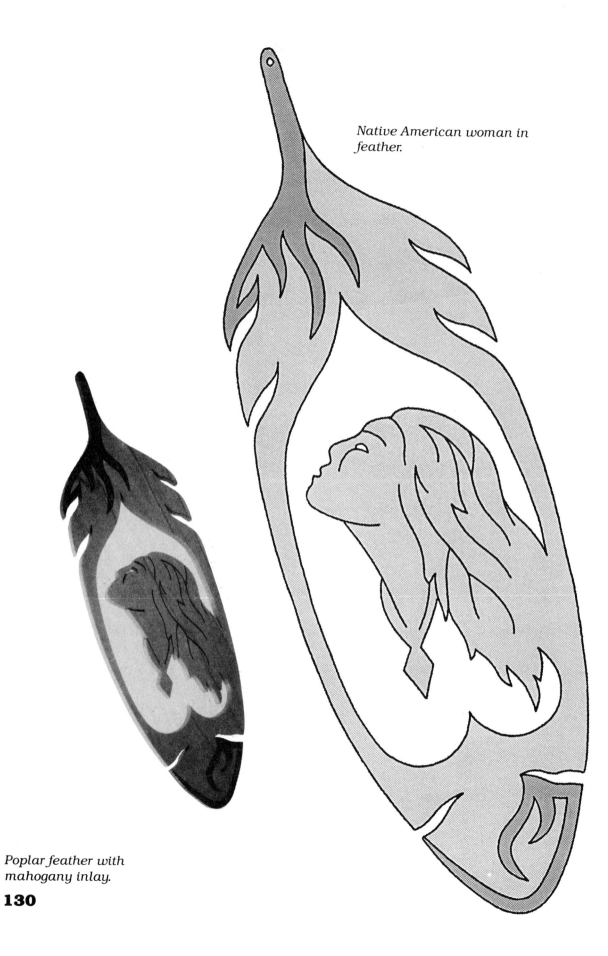

Native American woman in feather.

Poplar feather with mahogany inlay.

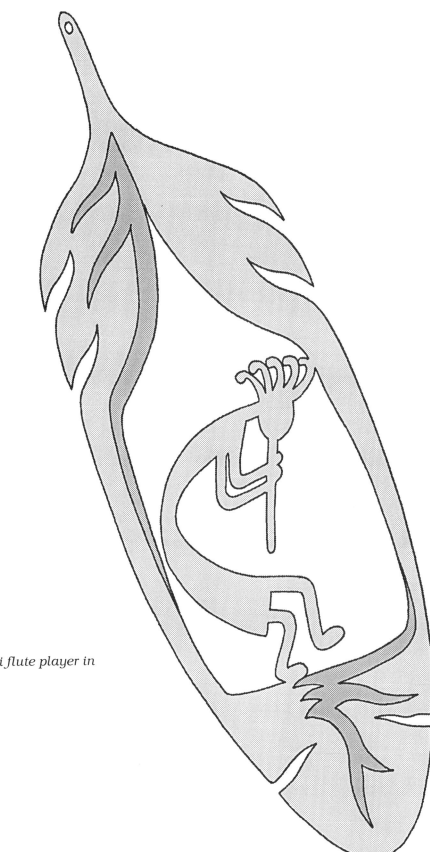

Kokopelli flute player in feather.

131

Lizards, Snake, and Toad

*Acid-treated copper lizard
with bright copper inlay.*

Lizard.

Lizard variations.

134

Double lizards.

135

Rattlesnake.

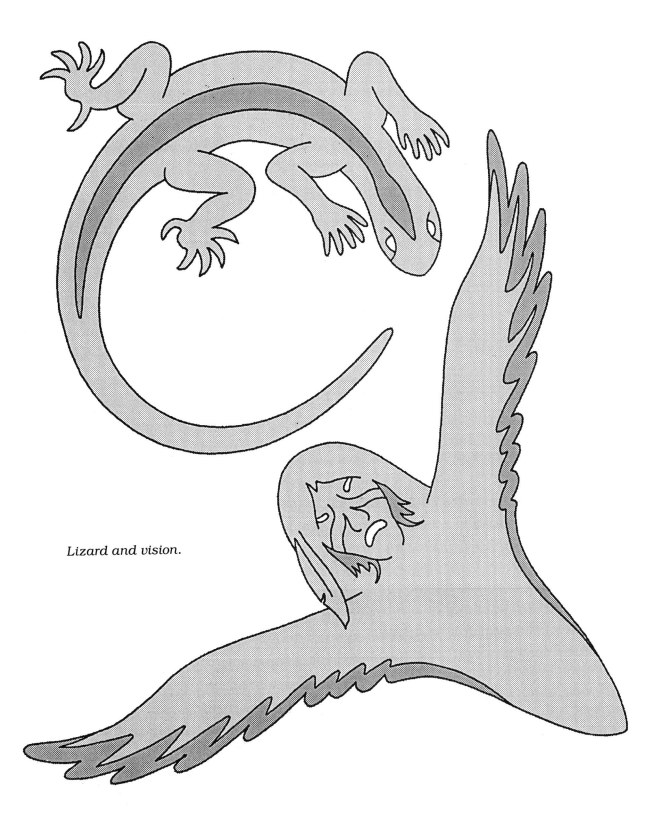

Lizard and vision.

Horned toad.

Pottery

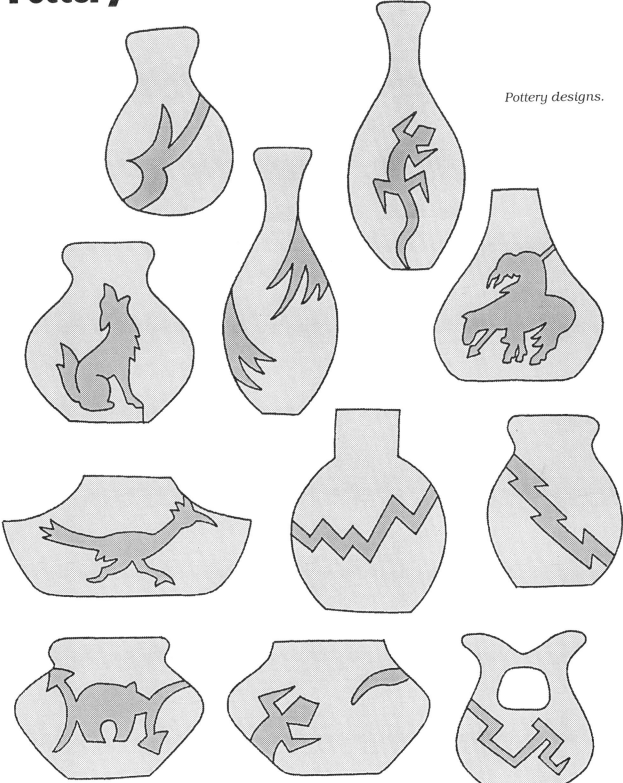

Pottery designs.

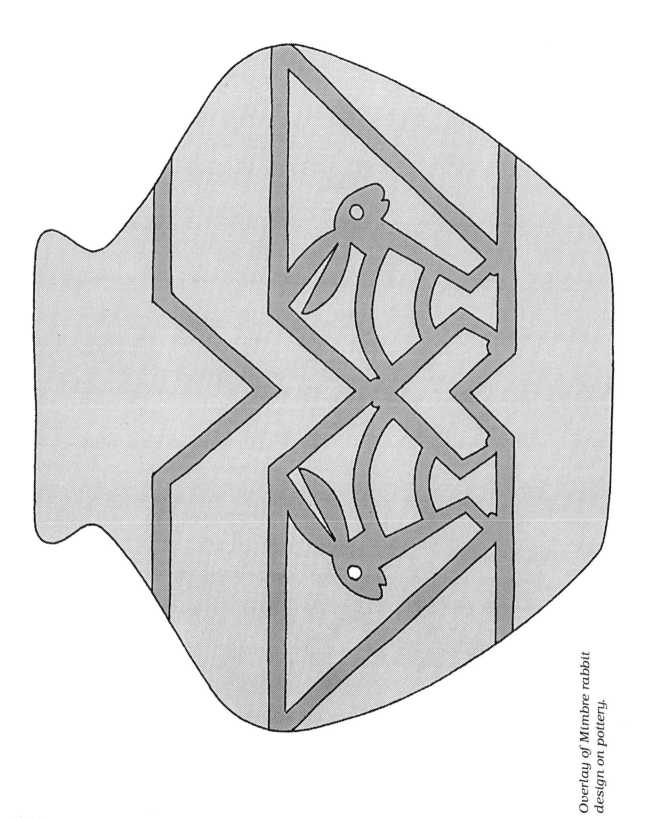

Overlay of Mimbre rabbit design on pottery.

*Flocked-plywood pot
accentuated with painted
overlay and feather
decoration.*

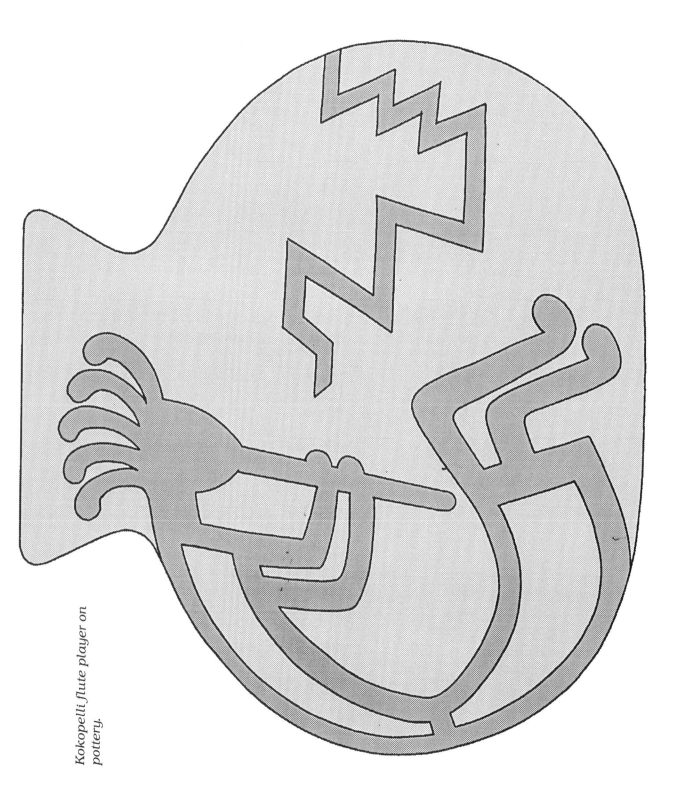

Kokopelli flute player on pottery.

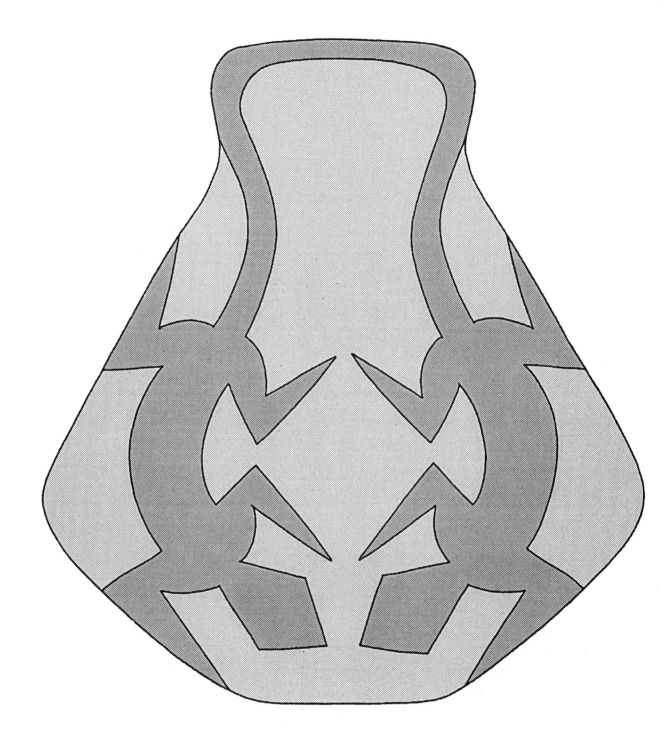

Lizards on pottery.

Coyote on pottery.

Another coyote on pottery.

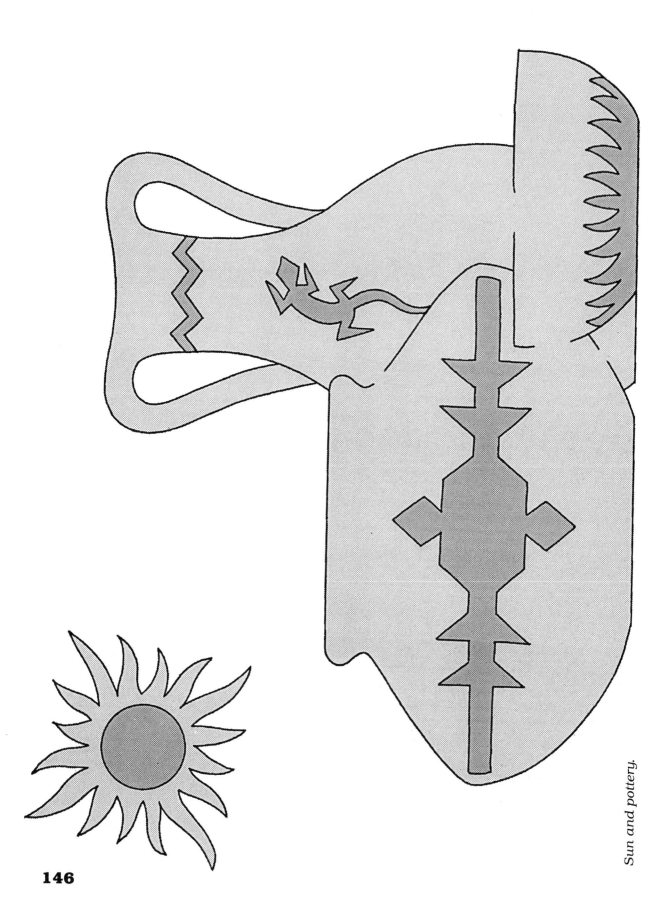

Sun and pottery.

Mimbre Designs

The following group of patterns features original designs of the Mimbre Native Americans. The Mimbres lived in the southwestern corner of what is now New Mexico from around the first to the eleventh centuries. Located along the banks of the Mimbre River, this great Native American nation developed brilliant means of artistic expression unlike those of any other Native American tribe. Using only materials provided by nature, the Mimbres painted their designs on the insides of clay bowls. They created countless designs featuring animals, people, ceremonies, landscapes, and even such events as childbirth, hunting, and insects being eaten by birds. Although they lived more than one thousand years ago, their artwork lives on and inspires many artists today.

This Mimbre lizard design sawn of ¹⁄₁₆″-thick plywood and stained is used as an overlay on a napkin/letter holder of natural ash.

Mimbre designs: lizard, rabbit with cat-like tail and flower, grasshopper, and rabbit.

Mimbre designs: quail, beetle, dragonfly, man with staff, and bee.

Mimbre designs: scorpion, cranes, turkey, load carrier, and fish.

Mimbre designs: rabbit, pottery pattern, and woman playing with child.

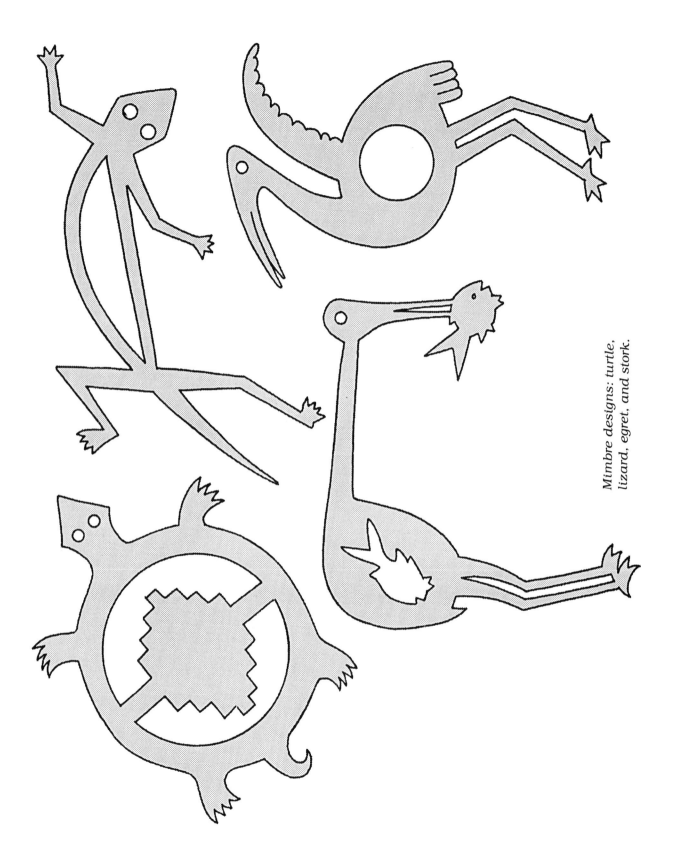

*Mimbre designs: turtle,
lizard, egret, and stork.*

152

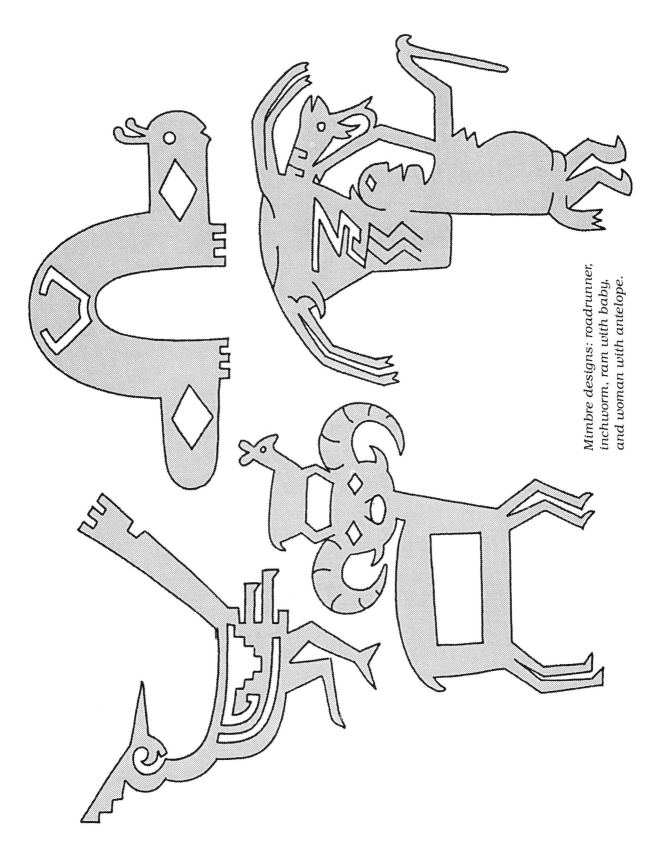

Mimbre designs: roadrunner, inchworm, ram with baby, and woman with antelope.

Mimbre designs: Kokopelli figure with bow and arrow, man wrestling a bear, and boys with bear cub.

154

About the Authors

Patrick Spielman. Expert woodworker and innovator, brilliant teacher and best-selling author, Patrick Spielman has used his rare combination of talents to write over 40 of the most popular woodworking titles—*The Router Handbook* (over 1,000,000 copies sold), *Scroll Saw Pattern Book, Sharpening Basics, Making Wood Decoys, Making Wood Signs* and numerous other pattern, project, tool, and technique books. As a master craftsman, he has also invented hundreds of ingenious jigs, fixtures, and other woodworking aids. A pioneer who has introduced scores of craftsmen to new and exciting avenues of woodworking, a technical consultant for tool manufacturers and for the classic *Encyclopedia of Furniture Making,* Patrick Spielman is one of the most respected authors in the field.

Dan Kihl. For the past fifteen years, Dan Kihl has been making a living with a scroll saw. Starting out in Wisconsin, where a friend gave him an old scroll saw, and needing products for his own gift shop, Dan combined his artistic ability with a love of nature and began creating his own innovative designs.

In 1989, Dan, his wife, and two children moved to Arizona, where he was immediately inspired by the area's natural beauty, wildlife, and Native American heritage. There he has developed several unique sculptural processes utilizing the scroll saw and materials that capture the spirit of the Southwest.

From his vast library of designs, Dan has created several highly successful products that have been wholesaled to the gift industry all over the country.

Current Books by Patrick Spielman

Carving Wild Animals: Life-Size Wood Figures. Spielman and renowned woodcarver Bill Dehos show how to carve more than 20 magnificent creatures of the North American wild. A cougar, black bear, prairie dog, squirrel, raccoon, and fox are some of the life-size animals included. Step-by-step, photo-filled instructions and multiple-view patterns, plus tips on the use of tools, wood selection, finishing, and polishing, help bring each animal to life. Oversized. Over 300 photos. 16 pages in full color. 240 pages.

Christmas Scroll Saw Patterns. Patrick and Patricia Spielman provide over 200 original, full-size scroll saw patterns with Christmas as the theme, including: toys, shelves, tree, window, and table decorations; segmented projects; and alphabets. A wide variety of Santas, trees, and holiday animals are included, as is a short, illustrated review of scroll saw techniques. 4 pages in color. 164 pages.

Classic Fretwork Scroll Saw Patterns. Spielman and coauthor James Reidle provide over 140 imaginative patterns inspired by and derived from mid- to late-19th-century scroll-saw masters. This book covers nearly 30 categories of patterns and includes a brief review of scroll-saw techniques and how to work with patterns. The patterns include ornamental numbers and letters, beautiful birds, signs, wall pockets, silhouettes, a sleigh, jewelry boxes, toy furniture, and more. 192 pages.

Country Mailboxes. Spielman and coauthor Paul Meisel have come up with the 20 best country-style mailbox designs. They include an old pump fire wagon, a Western saddle, a Dalmatian, and even a boy fishing. Simple instructions cover cutting, painting, decorating, and installation. Over 200 illustrations. 4 pages in color. 164 pages.

Gluing & Clamping. A thorough, up-to-date examination of one of the most critical steps in woodworking. Spielman explores the features of every type of glue—from traditional animal-hide glues to the newest epoxies—the clamps and tools needed, the bonding properties of different wood species, safety tips, and all techniques from edge-to-edge and end-to-end gluing to applying plastic laminates. Also included is a glossary of terms. Over 500 illustrations. 256 pages.

Making Country-Rustic Wood Projects. Hundreds of photos, patterns, and detailed scaled drawings reveal construction methods, woodworking techniques, and Spielman's professional secrets for making indoor and outdoor furniture in the distinctly attractive Country-Rustic style. Covered are all aspects of furniture making from choosing the best wood for the job to

texturing smooth boards. Among the dozens of projects are mailboxes, cabinets, shelves, coffee tables, weather vanes, doors, panelling, plant stands, and many other durable and economical pieces. 400 illustrations. 4 pages in color. 164 pages.

Making Wood Bowls with a Router & Scroll Saw. Using scroll-saw rings, inlays, fretted edges, and much more, Spielman and master craftsman Carl Roehl have developed a completely new approach to creating decorative bowls. Over 200 illustrations. 8 pages in color. 168 pages.

Making Wood Decoys. This clear, step-by-step approach to the basics of decoy carving is abundantly illustrated with close-up photos for designing, selecting, and obtaining woods; tools; feather detailing; painting; and finishing of decorative and working decoys. Six different professional decoy artists are featured. Photo gallery (4 pages in full color) along with numerous detailed plans for various popular decoys. 164 pages.

Making Wood Signs. Designing, selecting woods and tools, and every process through finishing clearly covered. Instructions for hand- and power-carving, routing, and sandblasting techniques for small to huge signs. Foolproof guides for professional letters and ornaments. Hundreds of photos (4 pages in full color). Lists sources for supplies and special tooling. 148 pages.

New Router Handbook. This updated and expanded version of the definitive guide to routing continues to revolutionize router use. The text, with over 1,000 illustrations, covers familiar and new routers, bits, accessories, and tables available today; complete maintenance and safety techniques; a multitude of techniques for both hand-held and mounted routers; plus dozens of helpful shop-made fixtures and jigs. 384 pages.

Original Scroll Saw Shelf Patterns. Patrick Spielman and Loren Raty provide over 50 original, full-size patterns for wall shelves, which may be copied and applied directly to wood. Photographs of finished shelves are included, as well as information on choosing woods, stack sawing, and finishing. 4 pages in color. 132 pages.

Realistic Decoys. Spielman and master carver Keith Bridenhagen reveal their successful techniques for carving, feather texturing, painting, and finishing wood decoys. Details you can't find elsewhere—anatomy, attitudes, markings, and the easy, step-by-step approach to perfect delicate procedures—make this book invaluable. Includes listings for contests, shows, and sources of tools and supplies. 274 close-up photos. 8 pages in color. 232 pages.

Router Basics. With over 200 close-up, step-by-step photos and drawings, this valuable starter handbook will guide the new owner, as well as provide a spark to owners for whom the router isn't the tool they turn to most often. Covers all the basic router styles, along with how-it-works descriptions of all its major features. Includes sections on bits and accessories, as well as square-cutting and trimming, case and furniture routing, cutting circles and arcs, template and freehand routing, and using the router with a router table. 128 pages.

Router Jigs & Techniques. A practical encyclopedia of information, covering the latest equipment to use with the router, it describes all the newest commercial routing machines, along with jigs, bits, and other aids and devices. The book not only provides invaluable tips on how to determine which router and bits to buy, it explains how to get the most out of the equipment once it is bought. Over 800 photos and illustrations. 384 pages.

Scroll Saw Basics. Features more than 275 illustrations covering basic techniques and accessories. Sections include types of saws, features, selection of blades, safety, and how to use patterns. Half a dozen patterns are included to help the scroll saw user get started. Basic cutting techniques are covered, including inside cuts, bevel cuts, stack-sawing, and others. 128 pages.

Scroll Saw Country Patterns. With 300 full-size patterns in 28 categories, this selection of projects covers an extraordinary range, with instructions every step of the way. Projects include farm animals, people, birds, and butterflies, plus letter and key holders, coasters, switch plates, country hearts, and more. Directions for piercing, drilling, sanding, and finishing, as well as tips on using special tools. 4 pages in color. 196 pages.

Scroll Saw Fretwork Patterns. This companion book to *Scroll Saw Fretwork Techniques & Projects* features over 200 fabulous, full-size fretwork patterns. These patterns, drawn by James Reidle, include popular classic designs, plus an array of imaginative contemporary ones. Choose from a variety of numbers, signs, brackets, animals, miniatures, and silhouettes, and more. 256 pages.

Scroll Saw Fretwork Techniques & Projects. A study in the historical development of fretwork, as well as the tools, techniques, materials, and project styles that have evolved over the past 130 years. Every intricate turn and cut is explained, with over 550 step-by-step photos and illustrations. Patterns for all 32 projects are shown in full color. The book also covers some modern scroll-sawing machines as well as state-of-the-art fretwork and fine scroll-sawing techniques. 8 pages in color. 232 pages.

Scroll Saw Handbook. The workshop manual to this versatile tool includes the basics (how scroll saws work, blades to use, etc.) and the advantages and disadvantages of the general types and specific brand-name models on the market. All cutting techniques are detailed, including compound and bevel sawing, making inlays, reliefs, and recesses, cutting metals and other non-woods, and marquetry. There's even a section on transferring patterns to wood. Over 500 illustrations. 256 pages.

Scroll Saw Holiday Patterns. Patrick and Patricia Spielman provide over 100 full-size, shaded patterns for easy cutting, plus full-color photos of projects. Will serve all your holiday pleasures—all year long. Use these holiday patterns to create decorations, centerpieces, mailboxes, and diverse projects to keep or give as gifts. Standard holidays, as well as the four seasons, birthdays, and anniversaries, are represented. 8 pages of color. 168 pages.

Scroll Saw Pattern Book. The original classic pattern book—over 450 patterns for wall plaques, refrigerator magnets, candle holders, pegboards, jewelry, ornaments, shelves, brackets, picture frames, signboards, and many other projects. Beginning and experienced scroll saw users alike will find something to intrigue and challenge them. 256 pages.

Scroll Saw Patterns for the Country Home. Patrick and Patricia Spielman and Sherri Spielman Valitchka produce a wide-ranging collection of over 200 patterns on country themes, including simple cutouts, mobiles, shelves, sculpture, pull toys, door and window toppers, clock holders, photo frames, layered pictures, and more. Over 80 black-and-white photos and 8 pages of color photos help you to visualize the steps involved as well as the finished projects. General instructions in Spielman's clear and concise style are included. 200 pages.

Scroll Saw Puzzle Patterns. 80 full-size patterns for jigsaw puzzles, stand-up puzzles, and inlay puzzles. With meticulous attention to detail, Patrick and Patricia Spielman provide instructions and step-by-step photos, along with tips on tools and wood selection, for making dinosaurs, camels, hippopotami, alligators—even a family of elephants! Inlay puzzle patterns include basic shapes, numbers, an accurate piece-together map of the United States, and a host of other colorful educational and enjoyable games for children. 8 pages of color. 264 pages.

Scroll Saw Shelf Patterns. Spielman and master scroll saw designer Loren Raty offer full-size patterns for 44 different shelf styles. Designs include wall shelves, corner shelves, and multi-tiered shelves. The patterns work well with ¼-inch hardwood, plywood or any solid wood. Over 150 illustrations. 4 pages in color. 132 pages.

Scroll Saw Silhouette Patterns. With over 120 designs, Spielman and James Reidle provide an extremely diverse collection of intricate silhouette patterns, ranging from Victorian themes to sports to cowboys. They also include mammals, birds, country and nautical designs, as well as dragons, cars, and Christmas themes. Tips, hints, and advice are included along with detailed photos of finished works. 160 pages.

Sharpening Basics. The ultimate handbook that goes well beyond the "basics" to become the major up-to-date reference work features more than 300 detailed illustrations (mostly photos) explaining every facet of tool sharpening. Sections include bench-sharpening tools, sharpening machines, and safety. Chapters cover cleaning tools, and sharpening all sorts of tools, including chisels, plane blades (irons), hand knives, carving tools, turning tools, drill and boring tools, router and shaper tools, jointer and planer knives, drivers and scrapers, and, of course, saws. 128 pages.

Spielman's Original Scroll Saw Patterns. 262 full-size patterns that don't appear elsewhere feature teddy bears, dinosaurs, sports figures, dancers, cowboy cutouts, Christmas ornaments, and dozens more. Fretwork patterns are included for a Viking ship, framed cutouts, wall-hangers, key-chain miniatures, jewelry, and much more. Hundreds of step-by-step photos and drawings show how to turn, repeat, and crop each design for thousands of variations. 4 pages of color. 228 pages.

Victorian Gingerbread: Patterns & Techniques. Authentic pattern designs (many full-size) cover the full range of indoor and outdoor detailing: brackets, corbels, shelves, grilles, spandrels, balusters, running trim, headers, valances, gable ornaments, screen doors, pickets, trellises, and much more. Also included are complete plans for Victorian mailboxes, house numbers, signs, and more. With clear instructions and helpful drawings by James Reidle, the book also provides tips for making gingerbread trim. 8 pages in color. 200 pages.

Victorian Scroll Saw Patterns. Intricate original designs plus classics from the 19th century are presented in full-size, shaded patterns. Instructions are provided with drawings and photos. Projects include alphabets and numbers, silhouettes and designs for shelves, frames, filigree baskets, plant holders, decorative boxes, picture frames, welcome signs, architectural ornaments, and much more. 160 pages.

Woodworker's Pattern Library: Alphabets & Designs. Spielman and daughter Sherri Spielman Valitchka have come up with a collection of 40 alphabets and matching number patterns in the new series the *Woodworker's Pattern Library.* Upper- and lowercase alphabets are presented for all woodworking uses, including block script, italic, and a section on decorative design elements to complement uses of lettering. An introductory section on Basic Tips provides information on enlarging and transferring patterns as well as on making templates. 128 pages.

Woodworker's Pattern Library: Sports Figures. Spielman and Brian Dahlen have put together a full range of sports-related patterns for the new series the *Woodworker's Pattern Library.* Sports images for scroll-sawing enthusiasts include over 125 patterns in 34 categories of sporting activity. The patterns can be incorporated in functional projects such as signs or furniture and shelves or they can be used simply for decorative accent such as silhouettes in windows or against walls. An introductory section on Basic Tips provides information on enlarging and transferring patterns as well as on cutting techniques such as stack sawing. 128 pages.

Working Green Wood with PEG. Covers every process for making beautiful, inexpensive projects from green wood without cracking, splitting, or warping it. Hundreds of clear photos and drawings show every step from obtaining the raw wood through shaping, treating, and finishing PEG-treated projects. 175 unusual project ideas. Lists supply sources. 120 pages.

Index